HOW TO FIX THE SCHOOLS

HOW TO FIX THE
SCHOOLS

*Educational Errors That Hurt
Students, Teachers, and Schools*

DR. CLIFFORD BEBELL

iUniverse LLC
Bloomington

HOW TO FIX THE SCHOOLS
EDUCATIONAL ERRORS THAT HURT STUDENTS, TEACHERS, AND SCHOOLS

iUniverse books may be ordered through booksellers or by contacting:

iUniverse
1663 Liberty Drive
Bloomington, IN 47403
www.iuniverse.com
1-800-Authors (1-800-288-4677)

ISBN: 978-1-4917-0955-9 (sc)
ISBN: 978-1-4917-0957-3 (hc)
ISBN: 978-1-4917-0956-6 (e)

Library of Congress Control Number: 2013917460

Printed in the United States of America.

iUniverse rev. date: 10/29/2013

CONTENTS

Preface. vii

Introduction ix

PART ONE   The Major Challenge. 1

                 1. Individual differences among students 2

PART TWO   What Do We Do Wrong? 7

                 2. Teaching as "telling" 7

                 3. Improper use of homework. 17

                 4. Inadequate treatment of reading deficiencies . . . 23

                 5. The ABCDF system of grading 28

                 6. Poor testing practices. 42

PART THREE The Challenge of Change 61

                 7. Moving the Queen Mary 62

                 8. The conditions which prevail. 66

                 9. The tie-downs 67

PART FOUR   The Process of Change 85

                  10. Goals and objectives. 87

                  11. Planning and conducting experimental efforts. . 99

                  12. Criteria for evaluation. 103

                  13. Evaluation procedures 107

PART FIVE   Changing the System 113

                  14. What do we need to change? 113

                  15. Five flawed practices 113

                  16. The curriculum 115

                  17. The program of evaluation 126

                  18. Organization of education 132

                  19. The teaching profession 140

                  20. Expectations 157

PART SIX   A Better School System 161

                  21. Fulfilling the wishes of the community 162

                  22. Meeting the needs of the students 162

                  23. Meeting the needs of the nation 164

APPENDIX   A Case Study: Critical Thinking 167

PREFACE

THIS BOOK SHOULD HAVE BEEN WRITTEN MANY YEARS AGO, WHEN I WAS an active educator, and saw much that I thought should be changed. Needless to say, I let the opportunity to express such thoughts slip away, and now I find myself picking it up, long after I've retired.

But as I converse with parents and persons active in schools, and read accounts in the press, I find that many practices and conditions I deplored years ago are still common. Indeed, I'm astounded at how little change has taken place in the last half-century.

So, many years later, and lacking intimate contact with recent research and experimentation, I find myself motivated to say my piece before passing from the scene. I believe I still have some valid insights, so I'll make one last effort to influence education.

But don't think I'm trying to say a lot that's new. It's almost impossible to do that in education. Everything has appeared somewhere at some time. All I can hope for is to collect relevant ideas, phrase them my own way, and hope to be persuasive.

I address everyone who cares about schools, although many suggestions are directed at teachers and other educators. But parents, and indeed all citizens, are a vital part of the educational scene, so I speak to them, too. I'll try to use plain talk, stay away from jargon and abstractions, avoid inflammatory remarks, and rely mainly on common sense and common experience.

Please don't prejudge my remarks because of my years. Ideas are ideas, and if they're any good, their origin is irrelevant. If they're no good, their origin is meaningless. Please consider mine with an open mind, and if you like them, use them.

INTRODUCTION

THE PRESUMPTUOUS TITLE OF THIS BOOK IS INTENTIONALLY CHOSEN TO attract attention, and perhaps to show a little humor (A very little?). I don't really think I'm going to fix the schools, although I do think that if my remarks are taken seriously, major change could occur.

The organization of the book is quite simple. First, I'll present what I consider to be the greatest unmet challenge in the schools—the failure to deal adequately with individual differences among learners. That is to say, the failure to meet all needs of all students.

Following this, I'll discuss five practices which I believe interfere with learning, and contribute to this failure:

Teaching as "telling,"
Improper use of homework,
Inadequate treatment of reading deficiencies,
The ABCDF system of grading,
Poor testing practices.

For each of these, I'll examine present conditions, and try to justify my criticisms. I'll follow by suggesting what might be done to improve matters within the present system—by teachers, by principals and supervisors, and by parents.

Then, I'll address major changes which I consider are desirable, and the impediments and other factors affecting change. I'll note strategies which might be employed, and how any serious effort to break new ground might be organized and conducted. Evaluation will be stressed at all times, and I'll try to detail how it might be done. I add an appendix intended to illustrate the bumps and bruises of a real-life experimental effort.

Finally, I'll present a picture of what I believe education of the future should be like.

Credo for education. Before I do anything, though, I should outline my views, so you can see if I have hidden agendas. All my suggestions will focus on items in the list below, which I call a credo for education. It has two headings: outcomes of education and principles of operation—what we should try to accomplish and how we should go about it. If something I write doesn't jibe with these, either I've made a misstep, or you've misjudged. I hope you can accept these core beliefs as a legitimate effort to ensure the best possible education for the most possible students.

<u>Outcomes of Education</u>

1. Possession of those aspects of our subject-matter heritage which are essential for a successful life as a citizen, worker, and member of society.

2. A lifelong love of learning and the skills and habits of problem-solving and critical-thinking,

3. The values, habits, and skills of a fully effective adult.

4. Physical fitness and good health habits.

Principles of Operation

1. Schools must help *all* students at *all* ability levels to reach their optimum development.

2. Student progress toward *all* goals of education should be guided, recorded, and reported.

3. *All* achievement by a student, however minimal, should be recorded and reported.

4. Moral behavior is to be encouraged and reinforced.

5. Nothing should impede the development of lifelong skills and habits of learning, critical-thinking, and problem-solving.

6. Constant attention should be paid to the attitudes and skills of good human interaction.

7. Evaluation is at the heart of education; all endeavors of students and educators should be examined to determine if they reach their objectives, and if those objectives have value.

8. To result in action, all evaluation must be accepted by the recipient, i.e., effectively become self-evaluation.

9. No student should be required to do anything beyond his or her level of preparation; teaching is effective only when learners are ready for it.

10. Programs should be provided for all with special needs, including college preparation and vocational training.

11. Parent and community support is essential; parents must be involved in all major educational decisions.

12. Those who prepare teachers or provide in-service education should use the same methods as they expect their students to use.

I hope most of you will agree that this list contains desirable elements. You may disagree with some, or feel some are more important than others, or are too difficult to do, too unreasonable to expect, or too expensive to be practical. Keep any such thoughts in mind as we go along.

Let us begin.

PART ONE

The Major Challenge

T HE CENTRAL PURPOSE OF AMERICAN EDUCATION IS TO EDUCATE *ALL* our children to the best of our ability—and their ability. And I do mean, *all*. The ablest should be challenged to the top of their talent, and not be allowed to drift into boredom and lazy work habits. Weaker students should be helped achieve to the top of their talent, too, and to stay in school as long as it's beneficial to them.

It's my position that we have failed to do this. It's hard to say which harms society the most—the wasted gifts of underachievers or the lost productivity of dropouts. Who knows what might have been accomplished by the former? And who knows how much the latter cost society in lost production, and the expenses they occasion later?

Any practice which encourages students to drop out of school is impeding learning, at least for them. It's hard to believe that we give up on as many as we do. It's hard to believe that dropouts have no capacity to learn or contribute to society. It's hard to accept human loss.

There's widespread concern for dropouts, as there should be— and not only for humanitarian reasons. This lost group produces a large number of drug users, prison inmates, and welfare recipients. They've forfeited opportunities to train for decent-paying jobs, and they may well produce children predestined to the same path.

Society not only loses their services and taxes, it also has to bear the costs of prisons, welfare, and drug treatment.

We've often failed to meet our responsibility to our best students too, by spending so much time and effort on others that we don't challenge them to their fullest achievement. These inadequacies result from the way we structure education and the practices we use—matters which I believe go against common sense and common knowledge. In short, we don't address adequately the extreme differences among students' ability to learn, and we often do things which even impede learning.

Again I say, I'm not going to be truly original. The professional literature is more than merely voluminous—it seems limitless. Anyone hoping to say something which has never been said before is practicing self-delusion. But when important ideas pass unnoticed, we must try again, and yet again. I can hope only that this time someone is paying attention.

1. Individual differences among students

We all know people are different. If this weren't so, we wouldn't be able to recognize friends or family. And the differences occur in so many other ways than facial features—height, weight, hair color, athletic prowess, artistic and musical talent, and many more.

Especially manifold are intellectual differences—not simply I.Q., but also factors like interests, ways of learning, aptitude for numbers, spatial visualization, verbal skills, social intelligence, and others.

In addition, children mature at different rates, so that not all of the same age are ready for the same learning.

If you look at the schools, with their fixed schedules, curricular strictures, and organization into classes, you must surely recognize that such arrangements can make it extremely difficult to tend to variations like those I've just listed. Often, it's simply not done. We frequently treat all students alike in order to keep a class together, perhaps requiring them to learn in ways which are uncomfortable for them, or inappropriate for their level of achievement, or simply to wait while others catch up.

I've heard all the arguments defending current practices—budget constraints, parental expectations, administrative considerations, need for group learning, and the rest. But I'm not going to tackle these now. Instead, I'll propose things to be tried within the present system. Later, I'll discuss greater change.

As we examine how schools deal with individual differences, the first place to look is in the classroom.

Individual differences in the classroom. Consider the teacher's dilemma. Faced with a room full of unique individuals, and forced to keep everyone busy at the same time, what is the teacher to do? Instructors who would like to help learners on a one-on-one basis often see it as an impossible challenge.

Many feel the only thing they can do is teach everyone the same thing at the same time. They present the subject orally, expecting students to ask questions if they don't understand, and they assign work which, although it may begin in class, is mainly intended to be done at home. And there are many variations.

Sometimes they have students report on the work they've done, sometimes they have discussion periods where students interact, advancing and discussing ideas, and sometimes they use class time for question-and-answer sessions or for testing. But fundamentally, they treat the class as a unit, with everyone participating in the same activity at the same time.

Many teachers, especially in the elementary school, do try to reach students with differing abilities, some by grouping them within the class and assigning different levels of work to each, others by teaching small groups separately while the rest of the class does seat work. Some try to increase the amount of class time devoted to individual student study, where the instructor circulates, providing help to those who need it. This approach might even reach the point of turning the classroom into a kind of lab, with all learners proceeding at their own rate.

We see less of this effort to individualize as we move into the higher grades. Subject-matter specialists see their course-content as prescribed, with all students to be judged by the extent to which they master it. But there are some other possibilities.

Some teachers do schedule time for special help to students whose homework reveals a need for it. This is difficult to manage, however, since the teacher also has to insure that every one else in the class is engaged in useful activities.

Classroom practices like these are called individualized instruction, and many suggestions have been advanced on how to address the needs of students individually. But there's much resistance to this. Many teachers have received little of no training in such instruction, and feel at a loss. The challenge makes them uncomfortable. Their nature may be to like organization, and they may feel that dealing separately with various needs is the opposite of organization. Faculty members often show such feelings through resistance to in-service efforts to change their methods.

Many teachers hide from the impact of student differences by the way they treat homework. They make assignments that they believe are appropriate for what's been presented in class. Then they rarely see the variation in time and effort students put in at home. And they may attribute any variation in quality of work turned to differences in work habits, home situations, or other factors.

If all homework had to be completed during the class period, instructors would quickly learn how much less time is needed by better students than poorer ones. They'd also see a lot of idle time of the part of faster learners as the slower ones finished. Such a situation of course could not be tolerated.

Since extreme differences can be concealed by having work done at home, many teachers feel justified in treating everyone the same way, making oral presentations to the entire class. But in doing so, they tend to direct their remarks to what I call the "great gray middle," often boring the best students and over the heads of others. Later, I'll have more to say about this approach, as well as about homework practices.

Differences within a class can plague a teacher, and lead to relative neglect of students at both the top and bottom. I admire greatly the efforts of those who truly struggle to reach learners at all levels of ability. They are the cream of the profession, and more numerous than we often realize. In the next few sections, I shall make suggestions for encouraging and assisting individualization, and avoiding the one-size-fits-all approach.

Individual differences in the school. Many aspects of a school's organization seem to imply that students are alike. Grouping them into classes for instruction, requiring specific curriculum choices, standardizing the length of courses and class periods, constructing buildings with little variation in room size. All these conspire to put students into similar molds.

Many of these conditions are based on financial or administrative considerations. It's difficult and expensive to schedule space and staff for class periods or courses of varying length, or give students additional time or special attention.

Many approaches have been tried. Courses have been divided into sections, with students grouped according to ability. Advanced courses are created for abler students. Fewer are offered that focus on review or remediation. Schools have been differentiated, with some vocational and some college prep. Charter and magnet schools have sprung up, devoted to students with specialized interests or levels of attainment.

These have a varied record of success. No matter how much effort is made to achieve a homogeneous grouping of students, there are still differences. Their magnitude may have been reduced, but some differences still remain. And so the challenge remains, too. Educators must face the reality that every classroom has variation among its members.

PART TWO

What Do We Do Wrong?

2. Teaching as "telling"

AT THE HIGHER LEVELS OF EDUCATION, IT'S CALLED LECTURING, AT THE lower, it's usually thought of as a presentation to the whole class, or at least a major part of it. The teacher stands in front, explaining some aspect of the subject under study. This is easy to do, presumably involves the whole class, and of course covers some element of the curriculum. It assumes everyone has an equal opportunity to learn.

But this is simply not true. It's virtually impossible to make oral statements that are equally meaningful to everyone who hears. Ignoring the fact that attention may wander, anything taught this way is usually too easy for the best students, and too hard for poorer ones. It's probably safe to say that any time all students in a class are doing the same thing at the same time, some are under-challenged and some over-challenged.

Yet, high schools and colleges are notorious for the amount of time an instructor stands before a group of students, telling them what they need to know. Indeed, for many people, lecturing is synonymous with teaching. I once visited a student teacher of English, only to find her wandering around the classroom, helping students as they worked on an assignment she'd given. When she saw me, she said, "I'm sorry I didn't know you were coming. If I had, I would have arranged to teach, so you could observe me." I had to help her see that she was intuitively doing something which was educationally effective.

I visited another student teacher on a different occasion, only to find her presenting Hamlet to a high-school class by reading from a paper behind a lectern—clearly the method her professors had used. The students were bored out of their skulls. Among other things, this is an indictment of the methods class she'd taken, which had been taught by a college professor of English. Many campuses permit subject-matter departments to control the methods courses, with the result that the practices of college professors may be urged upon future elementary and high-school teachers.

Consider the shortcomings of lecturing. The first is that the lecturer is the only person who is active. The students are engaged in passive learning, if indeed they're paying attention at all. We all know how hard it is to keep focused on a sermon, or a treasurer's report, or the reading of the minutes. We often find our attention wandering, and suddenly realize we don't remember what's just been said. Why should we believe children are any more able than adults to keep their minds focused on what they're hearing?

Every teacher knows that assignments which have been given orally will not be done by a sizable portion of the class, who say they forgot, or even that they never heard it at all. So teachers hand out copies of an assignment or put it on a web site. If they put it on the white board, they often insist the class write it down. Some go so far as to send a copy home. They feel this is needed to assure compliance.

So why do we rely so heavily on oral presentations to teach? Research, as well as common sense, tells us that we learn best when we learn by doing. Watching someone do something or being told how to do it never sinks in as well as doing it oneself. Yet we see schools consistently using an inferior teaching method.

Another shortcoming of the lecture approach is that it tends to devalue any textbook which is used. I once tutored a boy having difficulties in algebra. As I looked at his most recent assignment, it was clear he didn't have any understanding of it.

So I asked him if he understood the explanation in the textbook. He said, "I never read the book." "Why not?" I asked. His reply, "I figured the teacher had already told us in class everything that's in the book."

"Do you remember what the teacher said?"

"No."

But it had never occurred to him that the text could be of help.

So I walked him through the printed explanatory material, ensuring he read it carefully. Then, when we turned to the assignment again, he aced everything.

The lectures of many teachers reiterate what's already in the text. Isn't this duplication of effort? Why not have students read the book and work on assignments, with the teacher on hand to answer questions and provide clarification? Many have pushed this approach, calling for the teacher to be "not the sage on the stage, but the guide on the side." The Khan Academy represents one current effort to do this, giving students the opportunity to view lessons on YouTube, and encouraging teachers to help them apply their learnings in class.

A third shortcoming results inevitably from individual differences. I've already said that when everyone is doing the same thing, some are over- and some are under-challenged. Bored students and frustrated ones both stop listening. How can it be good education when a major portion of the class is mentally absent? And for the weaker student, the only hope is to get special help or spend long after-school hours hitting the books.

Fortunately, the elementary school has largely moved away from whole-class presentations, especially in the primary grades. But the higher one goes in the school structure, the more lecturing one sees. Many college professors virtually ignore individual differences, saying that their responsibility is to present the subject, or effort, with everyone grade accordingly.

What teachers can do about "telling." It may be virtually impossible to recondition teachers who have been "telling" students all their lives. They grew up in classrooms conducted that way, they learned to do it themselves, and to them teaching *is* "telling." Remember my student teacher who regretted she hadn't been "teaching" when I came to observe.

And this method seems almost instinctual. If I ask someone to help me learn something, the first thing he or she does is explain it, and if I don't seem to understand, explain it all over again. The thought that I should be observed trying to apply what I heard, or listened to as I repeated it back in my own words, doesn't enter the picture. And yet, my learning is assured only if I can perform successfully on my own. And evidence shows that the best learning occurs when the learner is an active participant.

Often, I have to ask some one explaining something to watch as I try to apply what I've heard, or listen as I try to repeat. Most persons respond positively to such a request, as they remember their own past difficulties. So I'll now ask teachers to do the same thing—to ensure learners are active.

It may be presumptuous for me to do this—to think I can say something meaningful to instructors of all subjects. My own teaching background was mathematics and science, with some contact in English and foreign languages. So, I may be less helpful to teachers of other studies. Also, my remarks may not be as necessary in areas where the basic instructional approach already involves much student activity, like foreign languages, art, music, P.E., industrial arts, or home economics.

However, many basic principles operate in all subjects and many challenges are similar for all instructors. Classes should be organized in a way which ensures that all students are learning at their own rates. I'll do my best to propose ideas which require little adaptation for different subject fields, and hope my readers will make allowances.

There are at least two ways to do this. The first is for subjects which are sequential in nature, with earlier learnings essential to later ones, like reading, mathematics, science, foreign languages, and other performance courses requiring practice. The second can be used for subjects, such as history, geography, literature, and the like, where earlier topics are often not essential for understanding later ones, and students' learning can range from superficial to comprehensive. English may have a foot in both camps, with the study of literature similar to that of social studies, while writing or speaking correctly is a performance challenge.

In the first situation, some students will be doing work which is either more advanced or well behind that of others. And even those studying the same material at the same time may need tasks of differing degrees of difficulty. This latter approach may also be used in the second type of subject mentioned above. For example, a history teacher dealing with the Civil War can stress dates, battles, persons, and incidents, or can focus on important issues and their relation to earlier and later events.

Central to any individualizing of instruction is accurate knowledge of each student's level of ability and achievement. Pretests can tell the teacher where each class member is at the outset. And all testing can be used in such a way as to reveal, not only the level of learning, but also the areas where the student excels or needs help. Without this information, the instructor is often just guessing what assignments are appropriate, and how effective class presentations are.

It's simply not acceptable to give an assignment which is beyond the student's understanding. If this is done, it usually means that something earlier was not learned. It's this prior something which should be assigned, and not what is frustrating the pupil. Often it's reading which may be at fault. Many subjects and topics are totally inaccessible to someone deficient in reading.

Remediation is essential for a student who's too far behind. But there's a limit to how much any one teacher can do. If a learner needs more help than the instructor can provide, the school must come to the rescue. Unless we're willing to say, "We quit," some form of assistance must be found. Unfortunately, all too often we do say in effect, "We quit," and allow children to drift on with D's and F's until *they* quit.

Here are some suggestions of what a teacher might do:

1. When making a presentation to the whole class, try to find how often it has not grasped by the listeners. Ask a simple question like, "What did I just say?" or "Please write in your own words what I just said." Looking at the responses might humble you, but it can help ensure learning by everybody. Merely assigning homework is not enough. You need direct feedback to determine how effective you were.

2. Excuse some superior students from having to listen to presentations which don't challenge them. Allow them to study in their own way, and report when they're ready to be examined. If they have free time, they can work on special projects you've helped them choose or develop.

3. Review material with any students who didn't understand it the first time it was presented. Have something ready for others to do on their own.

4. Prepare a list of special projects for students to work on whenever they don't have a current assignment to do. These projects should be of varying levels of challenge, and the teacher should help each student choose or create one.

5. Address the whole class at the same time as seldom as possible, and use the time saved for students to work on what they've learned. At least occasionally, have them do homework in class, so you can observe work habits, note areas of difficulty, and be available to answer questions and provide help. Anyone who finishes early can work on a special project, as I've just discussed.

6. Divide the class into small, homogeneous groups to the fullest extent possible, for purposes of common presentations, common assignments, and cooperative work.

7. Experiment with some class sessions which are completely set up as study periods, allowing you to circulate, observe needs, and provide assistance.

8. In classes with textbooks, make sure every student can read and understand the text, perhaps by using a simple open-book quiz. Those who don't understand it should not be given assignments in it. Those who do should be encouraged to learn from it. Much learning in life is acquired this way. Don't give students a chance to say, "I never read the book. The teacher told us all it contains." Students working on their own, or together in small groups, must be able to use printed material.

9. For students unable to understand the books or other printed materials being used by the class, find, or create, others which are oriented to the area of study, but which are written at their reading level.

10. Remedial work is essential. A student who can't do the work should not be assigned it. Instead, give simpler assignments, or ones dealing with earlier learnings. If this is not possible, urge the school to provide special help.

11. Diagnosis is also essential. You should be able to say what each student does and does not know, or can and cannot do. Assignments, observation, and carefully-produced tests can be used for this. A pretest should be used at the beginning of a class, to find out what each student knows at the outset.

What principals and supervisors can do. Much of the above is asking many teachers to change their methods. They may feel my suggestions are unreasonable, too difficult, or are even impossible in their subject. How can we get such persons to explore, with an open mind, difficulties and possible benefits with a principal, supervisor, or fellow teachers?

At this point, I could easily fall into the trap of suggesting that teachers be required to teach the way the principal or supervisor wants them to. But such an approach might well be seen as a threat to academic freedom—with disastrous consequences. Challenging the practices of teachers, who are assumed to be masters of their own classrooms, has long been difficult for educational leaders.

For instance, people who believe teaching is synonymous with "telling" may feel that anyone asking them do it less is asking them to stop the very act of teaching. I can almost hear them say, "If I don't give everyone the same experience, how will they all learn the subject?" So extreme caution must be used. It's remarkably easy to arouse resistance.

Teachers are like all other people. They don't like to be told what to do. If they are to change, they must do it of their own volition. Asking them to do so makes many of them think they're being told they're not good enough. And everyone hates that thought. Leaders need to seek consensus, and act as non-directive counselors, soliciting input rather than giving directives.

They have to believe, and help teachers believe, that change comes for everyone. New evidence, new insights occur to all of us, and if promising, should stimulate us to try something new The results may be better, or may be not. Even when an idea seems great, one can't be sure.

But the only way improvement occurs is after something changes. Still, new ways are challenging, and often create the ambivalence which underlies resistance. If individualization of instruction is to increase, those fostering it must be skillful, sensitive to teachers' concerns, and strive mightily to involve faculty in all planning and decision-making.

But even as I defend teachers' rights to make their own decisions, I believe principals and supervisors have rights too. And they have an obligation to make their views known. Still, there's a narrow line between advancing ideas and pressuring others to use them.

In brief, educational leaders should provide help and encouragement to every teacher willing to experiment, should involve everyone in the search for improvement, and must be careful about asking them to change or trying to persuade them.

Here are a few suggestions:

1. Brainstorm with teachers about the challenge presented by individual differences, starting with areas where student needs are clearly not being met.

2. If there's openness to an idea among some faculty members, create a study group to investigate the best possible procedures and make recommendations.

3. Provide competent in-service training programs for any approach which emerges.

4. Provide encouragement, assistance, and materials to anyone willing to experiment.

5. Encourage teachers to plan together, work in harmony, and share ideas and results.

6. Provide opportunities for teachers doubtful about a new practice, or uncertain of their ability to use it, to observe other teachers in action.

7. If some faculty members cannot support an effort which a majority of teachers is willing to make, arrange reassignment for them. This should be done positively, respecting their right to make a professional judgment, and helping them go where they won't feel pressured.

8. Keep parents informed about anything being attempted, and the reasons behind it. Solicit their support and encouragement at home for what the school is doing.

What parents can do. There's no group of citizens who care more about schools than parents. Their children are there. And much evidence shows that families who are more involved have children who do better.

Parents are also citizens, and as such, share the responsibilities of everyone in the community for decisions affecting education. After all, the community ultimately controls the schools. The immediacy of parents' contact and their level of interest are such that they have a major role to play.

In particular, they should have a role in the task of meeting the needs of ***all*** students. When it's challenge of dealing with individual differences, parents are right there. No one knows their children as well as they do, although they may not possess some of the insights of professionals. And they're deeply concerned that the unique needs of each child of theirs be recognized and taken into account by the school.

Of course, they have no real role in classroom procedures, unless these appear harmful. But such a problem is not usual, and if it does occur is subject to discussion and action unique to each case. But overuse of "telling" by a teacher can lead to homework difficulties, where parents do have a role. This is discussed in the next section.

Here are some suggestions for parents.

1. If your child can't seem to understand certain homework assignments, or spends excessive amounts of time on them, be sure to inform the teacher. The child's difficulty may stem from not understanding in class.

2. Your children are unique, like all the rest, and you, who know them best, should inform teachers and/or the principal of any characteristics which might be of special benefit or difficulty.

3. If your child develops a special interest, or undertakes a special project at home, tell the teacher.

4. All comments a child makes about school, especially strong likes and dislikes, problems and pleasures, are things which the teacher should know about.

3. Improper use of homework.

Homework has already appeared in this account when discussing teachers' methods. But I specifically want to address the subject further, since I believe its improper use not only causes many student difficulties, it often keeps teachers from identifying problems

The topic is a two-edged sword. Without a doubt, working on assignments at home or in study periods can help a student develop good work habits and time-management skills. On the other hand, an inordinate amount can create a burden and affect learning adversely.

The most common practice is for teachers to assign homework as each sees fit, without anyone being responsible for the total amount of time and effort any individual student puts in. Especially in secondary schools, teachers are likely to say, "An hour a night is not too much in *my* subject." This can add up. If four teachers feel the same way, a student would have four hours of homework that night.

Is this what we truly believe is best for a child or teenager? With thirty hours at school and twenty hours of homework, children might have a longer work week than their parents.

An additional consideration arises that involves weaker students. What a teacher thinks is an hour's homework might be two hours or more for them.

This first came to my attention when I was fourteen. Being fairly able in mathematics, I could usually get assignments done in 15 to 20 minutes. Then I discovered some of my friends needed two hours, or even three. Even at that young age, I was horrified, and felt it wasn't fair. I haven't changed my opinion to this day.

The homework burden, then, falls disproportionately on the shoulders of weaker students—and their parents. If the work can't be finished in an hour, the load can become monstrous. It might even border on child abuse. We have labor laws to protect children from being overworked. Let's not have the schools lead in violating them.

Teachers often don't fully recognize this extreme discrepancy in time and labor. Many children spend exorbitant amounts of time—if they're conscientious—while others get off more lightly. Some can feel so overwhelmed that they do the work carelessly, or "lose" it, or lie about even having an assignment. None of this is conducive to learning.

An additional problem is that homework may burden parents. And they often don't have the knowledge and skills to help their children, or they may not view the subject the same way as the teacher. There's also the question of whether a school should expect parents to be supplementary teachers.

The use of homework can have a major influence on a teacher's practices. One of my earliest teaching jobs was at the laboratory school of Ohio State University. On my first day there, I was told by the director, "We don't approve of giving homework. I'll ask you not to use it." To say I was shocked is putting it mildly. I had no idea how I could teach without homework. I'd always used it.

But I set out to try. I knew students had to be active in the learning process, and if I couldn't give them homework, I'd have to use class time for them to apply what they'd learned. This meant I'd spend less time on whole-class presentations. Further, I knew some students would finish before others, so I had to find something constructive for them to do once they were done. In the end, I found that following the director's request brought a revolution in my teaching. Which may have been what he had in mind all along.

Since teachers are the ones who assign homework, they can do almost anything they want to. But they have to recognize that the burden varies from student to student, and they must take steps to avoid extreme disparity. If they don't do this, or are unaware of how much variation exists, they're not tending adequately to the needs of everyone.

I hope I haven't implied that I'm opposed to homework. It's the mis-use I object to. Without doubt, students should learn to organize their own learning, build good study habits, and become self-starters. Homework is an excellent way to do this, under the nurture of parents and teachers. And many forms of communication between the home and the school have been created to coordinate their efforts.

There are many ways of controlling homework, and of integrating it into the classroom experience. I want it done thoughtfully, with full understanding of each student's challenge, and faculty agreement on a reasonable work load. Right now, its role in students' learning is difficult to ascertain or influence. And as a way to deal with individual differences, it must be viewed as a not-very-good one.

A school-wide policy on homework might result in some teachers changing their habits, as it did with me. However, proposing changes in the use of homework is a hot issue. Many people not only think that it's essential, but that it can hardly ever be overdone. They call anyone questioning it as soft on standards or unwilling to face reality. I've made my case, and if you think I'm wrong, so be it.

But for those who see some rationality in my views, I'll make suggestions.

What teachers can do. If anyone can do something about homework, it's teachers. They assign it, evaluate the result, and count on it to improve learning. Often, marks on homework assignments become part of a final grade.

What I've already said about individualizing instruction is relevant here. Assignments should vary among students, and some should be done in class. I'll add a few comments here on how to integrate homework into class work.

1. Examine all work that's turned in, to identify students who didn't understand or didn't remember something covered in class. Apply one or more of the suggestions I made about dealing with individual differences.

2. Ask students, or their parents, how much time they're spending on homework. Do this for a long enough period to make sure the information represents a regular pattern. If too much time is being put in, have the parents observe their child's practices, and report what they see.

3. Students who regularly require a disproportionate amount of time are having difficulty. They need help, either catch-up assignments or other remedial work. Otherwise, they're destined to a poor grade. It may be possible to give them alternative assignments, at least for a while.

4. If a sizable portion of a class report excessive time on homework. rethink your practices. Ask other teachers what they do, or provide more time in class for students to work, or both. Try to coordinate with other faculty members. No student should have to spend more than an hour a night on any subject, and certainly not five times a week.

What principals and supervisors can do. As noted earlier, leaders should exercise restraint. I won't repeat, but I'll reemphasize: caution, caution, caution. You want to affect practice, but you don't want to arouse resistance, or alienate teachers.

Here are some things to do.

1. Make a survey of homework practices. If there's variation, especially among teachers in the same subject field, encourage them to talk to one another and seek consensus.

2. Ask teachers to have students report their homework load, consolidate the responses, and distribute the results to the faculty.

3. Request a volunteer teachers' committee to create a policy regarding homework, to ensure that practices are consistent, and the amount given any student is kept under control. If the school already has such a statement, ask that its effectiveness be studied.

4. Solicit parents' thoughts, asking if they think too much homework is required. If a family doesn't think the amount is reasonable, their child's chances of doing good work are diminished. If many parents believe too much is asked, hold a meeting to seek mutual understanding.

5. Provide an after-school study hall, with a teacher available to give help, where students can do homework This is particularly important for those who return to an empty house, have parents who are indifferent, or a home that's too noisy and crowded.

What parents can do. There's probably no school practice more subject to parental influence than homework. The student works at home, usually with some supervision, and parents usually are acutely aware of difficulties. At the very least, the home should let the school know if things are not going well.

I'll make a few suggestions.

1. Do everything you can to make homework attractive—a regular time and place to work, freedom from noise, siblings, and other distractions, and a reserved space for storing study needs. Absence of any of these makes the work harder, and hinders the development of good habits.

2. If any of the above conditions is unfavorable, have your child go to an after-school study hall, if there is one, or perhaps do homework in the public library.

3. Have a planned schedule, and see that it's followed; make sure the homework is completed. If necessary, become informed of the specific assignments that have been given.

4. Maintain good contact with teachers, learn what's going on in class, and their expectations for each of your children. Plan jointly with them if there are problems.

*5. **Don't**, I repeat, **don't** do the child's work yourself. Every teacher sometimes gets material which is clearly the work of someone other than the student. This person is an enabler—one who allows the child to gain a benefit without earning it. Ultimately, the learner loses self-respect, as well as respect for the learning supposedly gained. As a parent myself, I know how your heart goes out to a son or daughter who's struggling, and may be in anguish. But for the child's sake, don't do it. If you do help, make sure you help the student discover how to do the work, but don't do it yourself.*

6. Report to the teacher any of the following: 1) excessive amount of time on any subject, 2) extreme anxiety over an assignment, or aversion to it, 3) clear evidence an assignment is not understood, or 4) any incident you feel the teacher should know about. I don't mean to suggest daily reports, but truly unusual circumstances should be reported.

7. Take an interest in your child's work. This is one of the very best ways to be of help. Knowing what's been assigned and how well things are going, and praising successful work do wonders in improving motivation. And good motivation is the key to all learning. Show your loving support.

4. Inadequate treatment of reading deficiencies

It's almost impossible to overstate the importance of correcting reading problems. Every subject in the curriculum after the primary grades relies on students' being able to read—some subjects perhaps more than others, but all subjects in some way.

And yet, we allow children with reading difficulties to stay in classes while greater and greater reliance is placed on books and other printed materials. Often, students are asked to read things they simply cannot understand.

The schools' basic approach to this problem is to expect the classroom teacher to identify poor readers and bring them up to an adequate level as quickly as possible. In practice, though, this is often not accomplished, either because the problem is too profound, or because there are too many other demands on the teacher's time, or both. It's the shame of the schools that they tolerate students' drifting from grade to grade until they either drop out after a series of D's and F's, or graduate from high school still reading at an elementary-school level.

Some schools attempt remediation through special tutors or classes. All schools should do this; but its cost is usually advanced as the reason for not doing it. But the eventual financial and human cost of permitting students to fall short of their best attainment is surely higher still. I'll discuss financial problems later.

I'll not dwell on this matter beyond stating that in my opinion no student who is a year or more behind in reading in the third grade should be permitted to study any academic subject beyond that point. If expected to do so, he or she will learn less and less, struggle more and more, and eventually lose motivation.

I realize this is an extreme statement. And I'm not advocating that such a student be left behind to repeat third grade. Repeating a grade is widely viewed as undesirable, if for no other reason than that it usually doesn't work. Experience has shown that such an approach impedes a child's social and emotional development to such an extent that more is lost than is gained.

We feel that children learn best when they remain with their age-mates and their fiends. And there are many non-academic areas where poor readers can be successful. But what should be done about their deficiency?

They must be given as much special help as is necessary to bring their reading up to par. Any part of the academic curriculum they miss in the process is more easily made up than the amount they lose by trying to learn subjects without the ability to understand written materials.

I know the cost factor enters here, but I'll defer that discussion for now. I'll merely say that the needs of these students are no less severe than those of physically and mentally handicapped children, for whom we've found ways to fund special classes. Anyone who must learn everything orally has an extreme handicap, too, since oral learning is typically ephemeral.

What teachers can do. Nothing creates a greater problem for the teacher than a poor reader. Difficulty in remembering what was said in class, struggles with homework, inability to review prior learnings, and frustration with written materials, including tests—all these contribute to a disinterested learner who possibly quits listening and finds unconstructive things to do in class.

Here are some things to try.

*1. Do **not** teach over it, which is what so many do. They give assignments in a book the child has trouble reading, and either leave him to struggle, or suggest he get help. (I use the masculine here because the great majority of poor readers are boys.) Don't ever give students assignments requiring them to read beyond their level. I know this is frustrating to hear, since it gives you more work and a greater challenge.*

2. Many teachers make valiant efforts to do help the poor reader— even giving as much one-on-one attention as one can in a busy classroom. It might be possible to work with a small group of these students, while the rest of the class does seat work.

3. At the very least, for any assignment, find or create materials which poor readers can read. This is vital for those a year of more behind.

4. Make every effort to persuade the principal to arrange special remedial assistance for all such students. The further behind, the greater the urgency.

5. Inform parents of the seriousness of a child's reading problem— stressing the effect it can have on future learning. Encourage them to discuss it with the principal.

6. If no other resource is available, help parents get information and materials about reading problems, so that they can at least try to help.

7. Tell them the issue is so important that if the school can't provide special assistance, they should make very effort to find it elsewhere.

8. Don't give up on trying to get help. NOTHING ELSE IN A CHILD'S SCHOOLING IS AS IMPORTANT!

What principals and supervisors can do. They should review what I just said to teachers, and give all the help they can. Many schools play dead on reading deficiencies, counting on teachers to help laggards improve to a satisfactory level. Sometimes this happens, but by no means even frequently. If it doesn't, something must be done, or the student is doomed to failure.

1. Provide assistance, through special materials, aides, or scheduling changes, to encourage and assist all teachers trying to provide help to poor readers.

2. Arrange in-service training for any teacher who wishes to know more about helping poor readers within a class situation.

3. Provide remedial assistance for students identified by teachers as particularly needing assistance. If this is felt to be impossible because of monetary limitations, look at my discussion of finances later in this book. At the very least, request the district to provide special remediation for problem readers.

4. Discuss the problem with the poor reader's parents. Explain its seriousness. If the school is unable to provide special remediating, urge them to get special help, if possible. You can even suggest they try to influence school authorities to address the problem. I know this sounds almost subversive, but the learner's need, and the needs of all such learners, is so great that an educator's professional commitment should compel him or her to do everything possible.

What parents can do. There's nothing parents should be more worried about than a child's reading difficulty. Don't believe it's merely transient, and that a good teacher will correct it. That could happen, but often doesn't. and it shouldn't be counted on. You should not only be concerned, you should be active.

Here are some things you can do.

1. Find out exactly what the school is doing about your child's difficulty, and ask to be kept regularly informed about progress.

2. Read to your child or with your child, depending on the latter's age, reading level, and motivation. If parents value reading and do a lot of it themselves, students are less likely to have difficulty.

3. If you feel that too little is being done, and you're not able to provide professional help, inform yourself by studying professional materials on reading, which you should be able to get from the school or public library. You might be the only person giving assistance.

4. Solicit the help of other parents, as well as friends of the schools, to discuss the special role of reading in the curriculum, and ask their support in trying to get more emphasis on it.

5. Request an opportunity to address the school board and/or the superintendent, to express your concern and conviction, and that of others, about the importance of remedial reading. Ask that it be included in the school program.

6. Volunteer to cooperate in any way that's appropriate, and show your constant interest and support.

5. The ABCDF system of grading

This topic is like an electric third rail of education. It can destroy anyone who touches it. The system has been around like forever. It's almost sacrosanct to parents, particularly those of abler students, and is second nature to many teachers, especially in high school and college. You may think I'm crazy to question it. But I hope you'll refrain from judgment until you hear me out. I believe what I say is vital.

The ABCDF system basically fails because it doesn't do what it's supposed to do, while it sacrifices countless students in the process. I'll look at these points in some detail.

What's it supposed to do? If you asked many persons, you'd get many answers. But I think most would agree that grades are supposed: 1) to show what students have learned, and 2) to motivate them to do their best. I'll consider the first now, and the second, a little later.

For showing what anyone has learned, the system fails miserably. Few people can agree on the meaning of a specific grade. For example, a B might represent a C student rewarded for extra effort, an A student penalized for loafing, or a "normal" B student performing normally. No one except the instructor giving the grade can really say what it represents, and maybe even he or she doesn't recognize all the factors at work.

Many years ago, William Wrinkle, director of the laboratory school at Colorado State College of Education (now the University of Northern Colorado) reported a study where a number of school-board members were given reports describing the performance of various students in several subject areas. Each case study described one student in one subject, with information about work habits, homework performance, classroom behavior, test results, and other matters. The board members were asked to assign grades to the students. The variation was monumental. Some even ranged from A through F for a single student. Over the years, other studies have reported similar findings.

In addition, even if a grade means the same thing to everyone, it doesn't say very much. It's like an academy award of an Oscar, which labels a performance but doesn't reveal it. To do that requires at least the showing of excerpts from the film. I once asked some parents how they'd like getting a letter-grade as the full report of a medical examination. I simply can't understand why parents accept a grade as adequate information about their child's learning.

What causes such great variation? Several factors do. The first is what the instructor thinks is important. At least four major elements can influence a grade: 1) how much the student knows about the subject; 2) how much progress he or she has made (this usually reflects how much effort was made); 3) the student's conduct in class; and 4) administrative considerations, like absences or tardiness, failure to meet deadlines, messy work, etc. Some schools even have a policy requiring a teacher to lower a grade if the student is tardy or absent a specified number of times. It's impossible to know what mix of these four factors go into a particular grade.

One illustration of how criteria can vary appears in how differently P.E. and arithmetic are graded. I once asked a group of parents how they'd feel if the P.E. teacher took the class out, ran them around the track, giving A's to the first few to finish, B's to the next group, and so on, with tailenders getting F's. They all agreed that this was unfair, and thought effort and participation were better bases for grading. They said, "Some kids are just faster."

I rejoindered by saying that "Some kids are just quicker." What they objected to was exactly what is done in arithmetic. Of course, most of the parents thought the situation was justifiable since they believed arithmetic to be more important in later life than athleticism. I have no argument with this viewpoint, but do say that if this is what we do, let's be forthright, and acknowledge it. Also, let's do research. What is the relative importance of the two abilities, and under what circumstances?

In addition to the four elements listed earlier, another can enter: the emphasis the teacher places on correct English. Many persons believe that misspellings, errors of grammar and syntax, incomplete or run-on sentences, or bad paragraph organization should be part of the learning in all subjects, especially social studies. Others say such a practice means students are graded twice, or even more often, on English usage, giving this subject a disproportionate weight. I take no position on this controversy, but do believe it calls for agreement among faculty members about the role of English competence in grading.

But there are at least two more influences on grades, the teacher's standards and hidden agendas. Anyone knowledgeable about education knows some instructors demand more than others. We've all heard students gossip about who gives easy A's, and seen them angle to get in that teacher's classroom.

I saw this issue clearly when I was supervising student teachers, who were learning their skills in public-school classrooms under the supervision of experienced and presumably highly competent instructors. I'd watch them teach and make a judgment regarding their effectiveness. Then I'd look at the grades assigned by their supervisors. I was often amazed at the difference in our two assessments. I was also often amazed at how differently two supervising teachers would evaluate two students whose capabilities I thought were comparable. I'm not saying my judgment was superior to theirs. I'm merely pointing out the variation and subjectivity in grading. It is crystal clear to me that instructors vary widely in what they expect.

Finally, there's the matter of hidden agendas. I'll illustrate this point with an anecdote from my college days. When I was a freshman, I took a beginning course in Spanish. Since I'd had several years of French and Latin in secondary school, I found the course fairly easy and aced the assignments, as well as the tests and exams. I confidently expected a top grade.

But, something happened. It was the consequence of the instructor's remarks at the outset of the course and the university's policy regarding absences. This policy allowed each student to be in charge of his own attendance, without having to provide an excuse for any failure to attend class. He was limited to fifteen absences a semester. If he exceeded this amount, he'd be in trouble, perhaps suspension. If he didn't, his grade would only be affected by any possible impact on his subject-matter accomplishment.

The instructor stated on the first day that every student's grade would be totally (and he emphasized **totally**) based on the assignments, tests and examinations he'd give. Being a naive freshman, and hating that the class met first thing in the morning, I took him at his word, and used my entire allotment for absences on the Spanish course. I was careful, though, to turn in all assignments on time, and I showed up for all quizzes and exams—doing well, as I said.

When the semester was over, I was shocked to receive a mediocre grade. I had the temerity to ask why. (Remember, I was an immature freshman.) I can still see the professor standing up behind his desk, pounding on it, and shouting, "No blankety-blank freshman is going to cut **my** class 15 times, and get a top grade!"

31

I've told this story many times in courses I've taught on measurement and evaluation, to illustrate a hidden agenda. It's obvious my instructor had a criterion he didn't divulge when the course started. Possibly, he didn't even know he had it until the unanticipated occurred. In later years, I saw other teachers doing similar things—considering something in assigning a grade that they hadn't previously thought of or mentioned in class. Also, in later years, I came to see how my teacher must have felt, and I could understand his action.

So is it any wonder, in light of the preceding discussion, that grades vary to the point where they have little value beyond pinning a star on the recipient's chest? Is it any wonder that I think we should abandon our present system, and develop new and better ways of measuring and reporting student achievement? I'll suggest a possible approach later in this book

Competition and cooperation. Grades are basically competitive, since they necessitate the comparison of students with one another, Many people use this fact to justify the system, saying it prepares students for the real world. I suspect many of you agree with this, and will dispute anything I say to the contrary. I hope, though, that you'll hear me out.

There's a major difference between competition at school and competition in the workplace. We don't see CEO's competing with janitors, doctors with shoe salesmen, or teachers with carpenters. As people learn their capacities and limitations, they tend to limit their competitiveness to those with similar capabilities. It's only in schools that we force followers to compete with leaders. It's only there that we force competition on persons with little or no hope of success.

I'm not going to take a position on competition in general. Friendly rivalries among persons close to one another often seem part of their pleasure. I myself have been a committed competitor all my life, and have enjoyed it. At the same time, as I matured, I gained more and more desire to work in cooperation with others;

We've all seen cases where competition has gone beyond the bounds of good human relations, and we don't want this to happen at school. It's easy for the grading system to lead to it, though, sometimes involving parents. The need to compete escapes no one. So we need to know what benefits it has. And what dis-benefits. We must make a determined effort to learn when it fosters and when it impedes desired outcomes.

Competition can be friendly or hostile, constructive or invidious, fair or unfair. We must ensure that any use of it in schools is positive and not negative. There is great need of research to determine how or if it leads to better education.

A final point should be made about competition for grades. It tends to discourage cooperative learning. Whenever a teacher assigns a group project, with students collaborating on an endeavor and everyone contributing, the issue arises of how to grade their work. Should all members of the group get the same grade, even if they worked at different levels of performance? If not, how should the teacher distinguish among them? Should the students be asked to grade one another? If so, how reliable would the results be? And how desirable is it to ask boys and girls to report on one another?

Because of such difficulties, many teachers are reluctant to assign joint projects, despite the fact that much planning, development, and research rely on this approach. And the ability to get along with others is an important learning. Indeed. it's frequently listed in employers' expectations.

How does the system affect students' motivation? The second widely-accepted purpose of grades, as noted above, is motivating students to do their best. There's little doubt they accomplish this with many learners, especially abler ones. But let's examine this motivation, and how it affects learning.

One thing teachers and insightful parents learn early on is that the system causes students to appraise everything in how it affects their grades. They're motivated mainly in the areas which have an impact. "Will that be on the test?" is a common question. If you say, "No," you can see the class relax, and pay casual attention at best. If it isn't going to be on a test, it can't be very important.

This attitude frustrates teachers trying to show that learning can be a joy in itself, and that lifelong love of learning is a worthwhile goal. I recall encouraging college classes to do supplementary reading to enhance some aspect of a course, only to find that a mere minority actually did it—once they knew there'd be no test questions on it. I refused to use quizzes to compel them, since I didn't want them to acquire the attitude that reading was worthwhile only to get a grade. I never fully resolved this dilemma to my satisfaction.

The essence of the above is that good students work hard to get good grades, and both they and their parents place great value on them. The downside is that learning is not valued for itself, but for its role in getting an A. Yet I see young people acquiring skills with computers and video games without this motivation, and realize how much learning takes place when there's a love for it. It's too bad we often fail to create this in the school. We must find ways to marshal the natural inquisitiveness of young people to gain this end.

What about less able students? I just spoke of getting an A. But what about boys and girls with no hope of an A, a B, or even a C? There's an underclass in the schools—a sad group of students who reap a perennial harvest of D's and F's. What about them?

The community likes to think that if they'd only try harder, they'd move up. But bottom feeders are already behind, and have to make up lost ground before they can even compete on equal terms with the others. There's no way—for most of them

Furthermore, moving up means someone else moves down. This is the effect of grading on the curve. Some have to do badly. As a practical matter, this turns out to be much the same group year after year—students destined for an unending series of D's and F's.

There's little doubt these boys and girls feel the school doesn't care about them. They often become discouraged, and drop out. I would, too, if I were in their shoes. So I say that the system sacrifices the future of some students to reward and motivate the others.

I once taught a class in first-year Algebra, only to discover that some members didn't know enough arithmetic to do it. Yet I wanted to do something besides simply waiting for them to fail. So I got some arithmetic workbooks, and helped them work their way through them, then arranged for them to get credit for General Mathematics. If I hadn't done this, they'd all have gotten F's in Algebra. I was rewarded by one boy saying to me, "Mr. Bebell, you're the first teacher I've ever had who cared whether I learned or not."

This story points to my belief that we must do more for our weaker students. Clearly, grades don't motivate if there's little realistic hope for improvement. Indeed, they motivate in reverse. A succession of bad report cards convinces such young people to quit school.

Many experimental efforts exist to help students worn down by the system, and avert dropouts. We do counseling and provide special programs. But they still have to perform within the system, and often feel we're simply trying to get them accept the reality of bad grades.

We pay a terribly high price for the grading system—in both dollars and human suffering. If good grades are to be meaningful, bad grades must exist, and so we sacrifice a portion of our youth. Perhaps this could be tolerated (while seeking improvements) if the grading system did the job it's supposed to do. I've tried to show that it doesn't.

Using grades. Not only are grades problematic in themselves, they're used in questionable ways. For example, they're combined into grade-point averages (GPA's), sometimes calculated to two and three decimal points in order to determine awards and honors. If the original grades had been the results of opinion polls, a margin of error would have been noted, within which all results should be considered equal. How can schools accept finer distinctions than the original data justify statistically? This refusal to face the reality of subjectivity is demonstrated by those who think of themselves as models of intellectual integrity.

There's another usage that is also a mistake in my opinion. Consider the student who fails a course, only to retake it later, and get a better grade. Should his F be replaced with a B (or whatever) on his transcript, or should the two be averaged together? When I was active some years age, the customary procedure was to average the two. This may have changed, at least partly, in the years since, but I've not seen nor heard anything to make me think it has. I believe that if you follow an earlier effort with a more successful one, the new grade should replace the first. Otherwise, the transcript misrepresents the student's eventual performance. Justifications for averaging the two based on consideration of course load, graduation requirements, or other matters miss the point.

Use by colleges and employers. My final area of concern regarding the grading system is its supposed benefits in college admission and applications for employment. Many, if not most, parents believe that good grades are vital for getting a good job or entering a made good college.

The fact is that both employers and colleges don't pay as much attention to grades as parents may think. It's widely known that they're unreliable. As a result, many employers use a transcript primarily to get an idea of how smart and hardworking an applicant is. They see little correlation between what the student studied, and what his/her job will require—with the possible exception of the ability to write and speak good English, and perhaps some minimal skill in computation.

College personnel responsible for admissions also don't make great use of transcripts. They look at them mainly to see what subjects the student has taken. The principal grading statistic they consider is rank-in-class—a rough estimate of the applicant's aptitude and work habits, as compared with classmates.

Admissions officers simply don't trust the ability and objectivity of those who created the grades they see. They also note great variation in the practices of different schools. Therefore, they rely more on test results, out-of-school activities, letters of reference, and the applicant's own written words to help them choose entering freshmen.

Summary. The grading system has much on its plate. Its data are doubtful, it can lead to undesirable competition, it encourages many students to drop out of school, and it's not much used by colleges and employers. Not only does it sacrifice a portion of the school population, it has to answer for many outcomes which are at least questionable.

If you think I imply a need to rethink the system, you're absolutely right. In my opinion, it's responsible for some of the worst defects of education. Yet, it's still prevalent, especially at the higher levels.

You might suppose this lengthy diatribe reflects a reluctance on my part to work within the present system. But I believe in facing reality, and present practice is not going away any time soon. We have to live with it, and I'll do my best to suggest ways to avoid the worst.

What teachers can do. Teachers can do the most. After all, they give the grades. Indeed, the task is often viewed as the epitome of a teacher's job, with remarks like "She's a tough grader" or "He's an easy A."

Here are some recommendations.

1. You should be able to say what goes into any grade you give—subject-matter achievement, amount of growth and effort, classroom behavior, as well as the relative weight of each. I leave it to your judgment to decide the elements and their emphases. But you should be able to state them clearly and apply them fairly and consistently

2. If you allow anything other than level of subject-matter performance to affect a grade, you should justify your choice to the students and their parents.

3. If administrative factors, like absence or truancy, affect a grade, both students and parents should know. But do everything you can to keep such factors out, since they're presumed to carry their own penalty through a lowered ability to learn. If the student can do the work anyway, so be it. Administrative deductions are basically a punishment for behavior, and may well result in an inaccurate report of achievement.

4. Be careful about letting your feelings creep in, like being too easy on a student you like, or too hard on one you don't, or doing the reverse as you try to avoid partiality. Similarly, handle grades given to minorities carefully, making sure no bias—either way—enters in. Emotionality can sometimes be very subtle, so self-awareness is crucial.

5. Avoid giving failing grades, if at all possible. An F implies the student has learned nothing at all, and this is rarely true. It also paves the way for the recipient to quit school. Sometimes a grade of "Incomplete," possibly with a recommendation for remediation during the summer, is appropriate. Even giving no grade at all is better than an F, if you're allowed to do this.

6. Any grade which surprises and disappoints either students or their parents should be explained. It may affect future achievement adversely unless both see it as valid. Try to provide advance warnings, so that it doesn't come unexpectedly.

7. Evaluation is effective only after it's accepted by the student; in effect, it has to become self-evaluation. You should help students learn to judge their own efforts.

What principals and supervisors can do. Outsiders are in a poor position for judging a teacher's grades. In this connection, I'd like to tell another story.

I was conducting a course on educational measurement, when a junior high school principal asked what I thought he should do about one of his teachers. It was a young man, in his first year, who had devised the following method of grading for his Latin course. He assigned 100 points to each student at the beginning of the year, told them one point would be deducted for each mistake made, and a passing grade at midterm would be 70. When midterm came, 80 percent of the class were failing.

The class didn't have that many bad students. Their other grades proved that. It was obvious that an inexperienced teacher had made the poor choice of punishing mistakes rather than rewarding achievement, as well as not knowing how many mistakes a normal class would likely make.

The principal felt he had neither the right nor the knowledge to change the grades himself. Further, he believed it was not professionally proper to coerce the teacher, or even tell him he'd showed bad judgment. Still, he was reluctant to have the results sent to parents.

Fortunately, the young man resolved the issue by himself. He recognized he'd presented an inaccurate picture. So he gave everyone an in-progress status at midterm, and installed a plan for rewarding positive work. He clearly handled the matter professionally, thereby taking his principal off the hook. But the story shows the dilemma a principal can have when a teacher's grades are suspect. It also shows how delicate the issue can be, and how carefully one must tread.

What was said earlier about trying to change behavior certainly applies here. Any criticism of grades may be totally unacceptable to the teachers giving them. They may view it as an indictment of their professional competence. At the same time, inconsistencies, especially among teachers in the same subject field, are a problem which has to be faced.

I'll present a few thoughts for educational leaders.

1. Challenge the teachers of a specific subject area to agree on a consistent approach to grading, including the relative emphasis on the various factors involved and the criteria used to assess them.

2. Use a faculty meeting to address the question of ensuring that grades are truly meaningful to anyone reading a transcript. Specifically discuss the role of such matters as English usage, neatness, and student behavior.

3. Ask a volunteer group of teachers to study and make recommendations about the information which should accompany a grade.

4. Prepare case studies describing students' performance on tests, assignments, and in class, and ask teachers to assign grades, discussing any differences which appear.

5. Give a group of parents and/or other community members the grades of the (unnamed) students who received them, asking what these are telling them. Prepare a response form for them to record their thoughts, and compare the results. Share findings with your teachers.

6. Ask a group of parents what they want to know about their children's achievements beyond what the report card normally tells them.

7. Ask a volunteer group of students to state in writing if they thought their grades were assigned fairly, and what they learned from them that was helpful. The process must be carefully conducted in a way that preserves anonymity.

8. Ask volunteer teachers to write a 25-50 word statement on each of their students, specifically suggesting what they need to do. Presumably, this could be sent home with the report card.

What parents can do. Parents have great emotional involvement in their children's grades. For many, they're the one thing they feel most strongly about, believing as they often do that good transcripts lead to good colleges. I'm surprised, though, that families make grades an end in themselves, without insisting on more and better information. When I asked about a B-plus for a doctor's examination, they were horrified.

I have a few comments to make.

1. Ask the teacher for an interpretation of a grade. What does it mean for the future? What did the child do well? What poorly? What should the parent be doing? Report cards should be taken to parent-teacher conferences, and questions of this kind raised.

2. Make written notes of all information obtained this way, so it can be consolidated in any future statements accompanying transcripts. If acceptable to the teacher, remarks might be recorded—to underscore their importance and ensure their accuracy.

3. Compare the grades of different teachers, and discuss any variance with them, or if not feasible, with the principal. Varying performance among subjects reveals a lot about the child—interests, abilities, learning difficulties. Ask for explanations, and any implications for future learning. All who work with a child should have access to this information.

4. Discuss with your children the grades they've received. It's important that each one feels treated fairly, and sees clearly what to do. If a child rejects a grade, the issue must be addressed cooperatively with the teacher, and resolved in a way which will enable the student to move ahead.

5. Avoid overemphasis on grades, which can create too much pressure. If the grade is low, in spite of the child having done his or her best, the job of everyone is to accept it, and work for improvement. This may require special help from the school. If the grade represents work which was not the student's best, there should a calm discussion of what happened, and joint child-parent-teacher plans made on how to improve.

6. Poor testing practices

Two kinds of tests are in common use today—those prepared by the classroom teacher and those obtained from outside sources. In my opinion, both are used badly. The former are poorly prepared and unreliable, while the latter are used to benefit administrators and politicians rather than instructors and students. I shall discuss the effectiveness of both kinds.

Teacher-made tests. Teachers have tested since time immemorial. They lecture and then test to find out what students have learned. They hand out books to read, and test to make sure they're read. They give assignments and grade the results—a form of testing. Usually, all grades they assign are based, at least partly, on tests and exams they've prepared. Indeed, many see these as so essential for learning as to render education unthinkable without them. They say students will not read or study or do serious work unless they know they'll be tested. For them, a major task of testing is motivating.

Still, for most people, the most commonly accepted purpose is to ascertain and record what a student has learned. Even those who stress its role as a motivator usually agree. And I believe it too. But this simple answer hides more than it reveals.

What do we expect students to learn? In other words, what should a test emphasize? Is it remembering information, understanding concepts, or demonstrating skills? Many people will say, all of them. And of course there's merit to this. But if one has forgotten a concept, the test reveals that fact alone. True learning is too complex to be determined this way.

Often, when a student produces an incorrect answer, what's revealed is unclear. It may be failure to remember, lack of skill, poor understanding, or some combination thereof. It says nothing about what the test-taker might have demonstrated if allowed to use a resource. Many teachers deal with this issue by using open-book exams to determine students' ability to use skills or apply concepts. Then, they test their ability to remember in a test for that purpose alone. Each of these aspects must be assessed separately if every student's unique needs are to be met.

Our present practice may well block students' maximum performance. Engineers would never think of applying their professional expertise on a major project without consulting resources and/or colleagues. Only in school examinations do we require that this not be done. I know it's essential to isolate what each student knows and doesn't know, so his or her achievement can be properly assessed. Nonetheless, we do this in a different context from that in which the achievement will be needed later and evaluated later.

Every item on an exam should be examined to determine what kind of learning it represents, and test makers should be wary of relying too heavily on memory. There's an old saying. "Education is what remains after you've forgotten everything you were taught." Memorized information is fragile and ephemeral, and quickly vanishes. Who among us could pass a physics test today which we'd taken successfully in high school? The results of many teacher-made tests are skewed by too many memory challenges, and fail to yield the best information about significant learning. Though they often also stress understanding and skills, they allow memory to guard the gate.

One effect of this is the temptation to make tests more difficult by increasing the burden of factual information. I've known teachers to scour the textbook for obscure facts, or even use footnotes, for test items. Is that making standards higher? I think not.

Of course, it's important to carry some items of information around with us, especially in language and computation. But many are readily retrievable. At one time, we relied upon dictionaries, atlases, and encyclopedias for this. Now it's the internet. Not a day passes without my Googling something, or using Wikipedia. Which probably reveals how little I use more advanced searches.

But a lifelong habit of using resources to retrieve information is not a rift in one's learning. Instead, it's a way to use knowledge confidently, and might well be called a form of continued learning. I refuse to acknowledge that my usage is evidence of inadequate education.

Validity of teachers' tests. The simple truth is that most teachers don't know much about test construction. They don't seem to understand the concepts of validity and reliability, or how to demonstrate them in an exam they've created. I'm not going to give a short course in test construction at this point, but will say that validity means that a test really does measure what it says it does. And reliability means that whatever it measures, it does so with confidence that it would regularly yield comparable results with similar students in similar situations. The first is like choosing the right tool for a carpentry task, and the second is knowing the tool will not break or fail to perform.

Teachers don't do the job of validation very well. They usually assume that any reasonable assortment of questions in a test is adequate, as long as they're spread over the full body of the subject field. This is a valid concept, but only if the distribution of items is wide enough, and they're randomly selected.

Usually this is not done. The teacher's judgment alone determines which pieces of information and understanding will be used. As a result, classroom tests are uncomfortably subjective, including the so-called objective tests (called objective, because all answers are either right or wrong and are often just check marks). They typically don't reflect the best practice.

I once had a professor in college, all of whose questions on the final exam focused on a single topic which he had covered in just one-half of one class-session—out of a total of 30—as a later review of my notes revealed.

In another incident from my college past, I faced the final examination with trepidation, since I hadn't studied very hard or very often, and there was much I didn't know. When I looked at the test, I discovered that there were eight questions, in four pairs, and we could choose to answer either one in each. To my amazement, and obvious delight, each pair included one topic I knew well and one I didn't. Because of this anomaly, I scored well in a course where I truly deserved a mediocre grade. The failure of the examination to reflect all major aspects of the subject created this opportunity.

So the test maker's choices may favor some learners more than others. Yet I've rarely seen teachers systematically compare the items on a test with the contents of the course or syllabus, to ensure that the latter is fairly represented, with the same relative emphasis on topics, procedures, and understanding as occurred in class.

Any disconnect between the content of a test and the content of the course in which it's used constitutes at least a partial breach in its validity. In most classrooms this is not serious, since the same person creates the test and teaches the course. But note my two stories, showing that a breach can widen to the point of misrepresentation of a student's performance.

Reliability of teachers' tests. Most teachers assume their mastery of a subject guarantees their ability to write questions that reveal student achievement. Yet I've seen few of them doing such simple item analysis as recording the range of scores on individual questions, to see how well the test has discriminated among students at all levels of ability.

Without easy questions, all poor students will score about the same, and without hard ones, all good students will do likewise. And without a continuum of difficulty, the test results for the class-middle will be somewhat catch-as-catch-can, and might yield different results if re-administered. A great deal of useful information about the needs of individual students can be obtained by examining the pattern of responses to items.

Unreliability results most often from poorly written test items. This happens frequently, and in many ways. One is simply poor language usage. It goes without saying that questions should be phrased in good English. So why do I say it? Because I've seen countless tests with unclear, ambiguous, or unfamiliar phraseology. To avoid this, everyone who has written an exam should have another person read it. Often, only a second mind can spot ways the language can misdirect, confuse, or baffle.

But reliability relies on more than item analysis and good English. A huge breach results from poor creation of questions to begin with. Another problem often arises in the way that answers are dealt with. I'll show a few of the difficulties.

Most teacher-made tests use one of three kinds of items: 1) objective ones like true-false and multiple-choice, 2) specific tasks to do or problems to solve, and 3) essay questions. The first of these is easy to score but hard to write, while the third is the reverse, easy to write and hard to score. The second is widely used since it seems to be easy both ways, but I'll consider its difficulties in a moment.

Objective items are widely used because responses are easily handled, but they're especially vulnerable to language difficulties. Not only because of poor phraseology, but also because of the fiendish difficulty of avoiding clues which allow a savvy test-taker to get correct answers by "gaming" the test, rather than knowing the subject. I was once able to get a satisfactory score in this way on a GRE exam in Biology in spite of the fact that I never studied biology in my life.

Too many teachers seem unable to avoid ambiguous language and the unconscious giving of clues. I've seen multiple-choice items where the test-maker copied the correct answer from a book, then wrote other choices in a style different from the author's. Some multiple-choice questions have appeared with the right answer noticeably a different length than the wrong ones. And I've seen matching lists which give clues to the correct answer to other items.

Furthermore, objective tests allow successful guessing to influence results. They're also much criticized by those who say that the ability to recognize correct material is a learning inferior than the ability to produce it from within. This, too, will be further considered at a later point.

Test-makers attempt to deal with this within an otherwise objective test by creating short-answer items. These appear in two forms, either direct questions calling for short, specific, right-or-wrong answers, or as statements, each of which contains a blank to be filled in from context. This latter type must be constructed carefully to avoid ambiguity, though, since they often produce unanticipated interpretations, and yield responses which must be considered correct. For example, the item, "President Lincoln was born in _____" (anticipating the response, ("1809"), might also be correctly answered with "Kentucky" or "a log cabin" (or even, "bed").

As we advance beyond objective instruments we find items presenting problems to solve or tasks to perform. These can still be right-or-wrong questions, and can come in a broad range of difficulty. They're much used in areas like mathematics, science, and foreign languages. The student is presented a problem which has one or more right answers and a correct way to do it. If instead, the question presents a task to do, acceptable results may vary widely, and will require judgment to evaluate.

Using problems as test items necessitate an agreed-upon procedure for grading results. At present, wrong answers are handled variously, with some teachers limiting themselves to full credit for right answers and no credit for wrong. Others, however, may require the student's work to be shown, in order to ascertain how many and what kinds of mistakes were made. For them, an answer which was done correctly, except for a single simple error, merits a score close to that for a perfect response. A specific effort might well receive different scores from different scorers.

Test reliability is severely affected by how responses are handled. The problem becomes doubled in spades when it comes to essay exams. This latter approach to testing is so important that I have given it a section to itself.

Essay tests. Dealing with higher forms of learning typically involves the essay examination. This presents specific challenges to students, who are required to write on them at some length, presumably revealing their ability to generate and organize ideas. Many people insist that it's the only true measure of learning.

Please don't think that prior exclusion of this approach from the discussion indicates my lack of faith in them. I too believe they have a significant role to play, and now devote this section to it.

Essay questions create a whole new ball game. They also constitute the bulk of many tests and assignments. It's easy to ask a student to write 100 words, or 200, or two pages, or whatever, on a particular topic or issue. What's not easy is how to assess the results.

Essays can be considered both as responses to be scored and as products to be judged. As can the performance of students in a classroom. But I'm reserving my comments about judging products and performance until later, when I consider evaluation procedures generally.

What makes essays so difficult to grade? To begin, examiners' subjectivity almost guarantees wide variation in the marks they assign. Essays can be ambiguous, confused, or confusing. Some teachers, in an effort to make grading as easy or objective as possible, compare answers to a checklist of what they believe should be included, without regard for anything they hadn't anticipated, or deducting for anything incorrect.

Those who do this rarely consider the integration, organization, or amplification of ideas, with the result that a student with lots of superficial knowledge scores better than one with deeper understanding of fewer issues. And it certainly leads to little or no credit for unanticipated, creative ideas.

There are almost as many ways of evaluating essays as there are teachers. Besides those who make checklists of what they expect and count how many appear, there are some who have an idea of how long a response should be and let length affect the grade they give. Others place great stress on careful organization and/or creative thought. They may let creativity and imagination offset some factual misinformation.

Many reduce scores because of poor English or messiness, but many do not. Possibly the greatest single cause of variation is how errors in English usage are treated. They go from being completely ignored to a major factor in unsatisfactory performance.

I go into some detail because many admirers of essay questions believe the results are the best indicator we have of how well a student understands a subject. And I count myself among them. The challenge to produce an integrated product which reflects the test-taker's learning is a true measure of understanding. It's unfortunate we have so much disagreement on how to judge the results. It's almost impossible to believe that any given essay would receive the same score from a variety of readers.

The challenge is immense. But it mustn't stop us. If we believe in helping boys and girls understand the subjects we teach, we must agree on desirable indicators of that learning and desirable ways of obtaining them.

I'll say no more, other than to note that teacher-made tests may be less indicative of a student's actual learning than their makers realize.

Improving teachers' capabilities. Teachers are very resistant to training in test construction and usage. I don't know why. But I often observed former students of mine in their own classrooms after graduation, and rarely found them applying principles of testing

I'd presumably taught them. Possibly, the explanation is that I was a poor teacher. But what about all the others I saw doing likewise? Most of them had been taught by someone other than me. Were we all bad teachers?

All I know for sure is that I rarely saw the use of testing procedures that had supposedly been learned. They rarely checked the validity of an instrument, and seemed even less concerned with reliability.

Possibly teachers are more influenced by the practices of their subject-matter professors or their student-teaching supervisors than by anything the education faculty might have done. I once thought that this could have been the result of an aversion to mathematics acquired in their early schooling. But I saw the same situation among algebra and geometry teachers. I was never able to decide why a reluctance to learn and to use techniques for checking validity and reliability is so widespread—especially with such a huge amount of information available.

Impact on results. Another issue which is seldom faced is the how the testing process itself might distort its own result. Students approach tests in various ways. Some are frightened, some race to finish, almost everyone is stressed. It's difficult to believe they all do their best work then.

The fact that exams have time limits (usually necessitated by fixed class periods) tends to increase the pressure. Many students panic as they see time running out, and try desperately to get something down for remaining items. Is this the way we want to assess learning—with a fight against the clock?

But even tests created to be too long to finish, with students being told this, and asked to go only as far as they can, don't diminish the stress, at least for some. I for one, as a test-taker, took such instructions as a challenge, and worked as fast as possible to see if I couldn't finish anyway, and prove the teacher wrong. Some students find themselves confused, and unsure of their best strategy—slow but sure, or fast and furious. Often, they start with one and finish with the other.

There are those who relax too much, take time to check answers, and end up not getting enough done to reveal their true level of learning. Variations in approach almost guarantee that a test result, presumably a measure of subject-matter mastery, includes an unknown error, based on the student's personality structure.

Finally, there are the savvy students who either learn test-taking strategies on their own or are taught them by someone. They seem to prefer outwitting the exam to preparing for it by subject-matter study.

So there are several ways in which an examination might fail to reveal students' achievement accurately. We must be aware of these and consciously and conscientiously seek ways to avoid them.

How does testing affect learning? There are at least two ways in which testing affects how students learn and what they learn. The first is that it reinforces their conviction that schoolwork is boring and uninteresting. Why else would teachers resort to coercion? And a second effect is that they'll focus on ephemeral and less important learnings rather than more important outcomes.

I often wonder why we have so much difficulty in instilling a true love of learning in schools when I see so much of it in other areas of life. Youngsters, and oldsters too, acquire high levels of skill in computers and video games without anyone teaching them. I've even seen kids texting from cell phones in their pockets. We obviously do something in our schools to turn off this faucet of motivated learning. That something is what I'm writing this book about.

I tried many times during my career to attack this issue. But I didn't have much success, probably because I was dealing with an attitude that was too deeply rooted. I sought to show my own love for what I was teaching. I'd encourage students to express their interests, so I'd know where they were coming from. I tried to help them see that what they were learning in school would help them in later life.

Still, when I'd give a reading assignment, someone would inevitably ask if there'd be a test on it. If I said there would not, but that it would contribute to their understanding, and they'd need it for class discussion, you can predict what happened. Usually, fewer than half did as I requested. The others must have felt they had better uses for their time, possibly for work with teachers who did use testing.

This is not the place to discuss what I did about this. A teacher does have several options. Rather, I wish to consider what those other teachers obtained, those who believe that testing is necessary to ensure that learners do the expected work. I can understand their point of view, since so many students virtually ignore anything which will not be on a test. But let's look at what they get.

These students are saying that passing a test is their first priority, with everything else at a lower rank. We've often heard of teachers teaching to the test, but it's evident that many, if not most, learners do the same thing. They study and learn what examinations emphasize.

This redoubles the teacher's responsibility to make certain that important educational outcomes are put front and center. But if instead, if a test maker places emphasis on memory, students will too. They'll focus on what they expect to appear on a test, and their concentration will be on remembering, remembering, remembering.

Cramming for an exam is all too common, although it's hard to believe this is motivated learning. It's more akin to motivated memorization. Crammers spend more time and effort on facts than on their significance. This is a focus on ephemeral learning. But no impassioned drive to gain knowledge quickly is an adequate substitute for mature, reflective acquisition of understanding. Students spend more time learning what they'll soon forget, and less time on what they should know for a lifetime. This is no way to engender a love of learning.

Now let me turn my attention to the standardized instruments used in testing programs imposed on the schools.

What about standardized tests? I say, imposed, because that is usually the case. State government or school administration wishes to determine how well educational outcomes are being achieved, often, although by no means exclusively, in reading, English, and mathematics. Or the federal government will link financial aid to evidence of accomplishment.

It was early in the twentieth century that tests were first created by someone other than teachers. In France, Binet created an instrument to determine objectively which children could benefit from schooling and which could not, and this has morphed into today's IQ tests. And from such a modest beginning has arisen the present-day megalith we call standardized achievement tests.

This development may well be one of the greatest achievements of twentieth–century education. Starting with a desire to find a way to identify promising learners, it's become a huge enterprise for obtaining useful information about students. We now have a vast array of instruments designed to measure almost anything you might care to name. I'll limit my remarks at this time, though, to those dealing with subject-matter achievement.

Since I devoted much of my career to the area of student evaluation, and taught courses on test construction and usage, you may wonder why I seem to imply that professionally-produced instruments can have an undesirable effect on learning. Certainly they're much more carefully prepared than those created by teachers. Their makers attack the issue of validity by using qualified specialists to select content. And no one can doubt their reliability, based on the care given to their construction, tryout, and analysis.

It's because of how they're used.

Perhaps I should replace the term, undesirable effect, with the more informative, "impede a positive effect." Early in my career, standardized tests were often used by teachers to identify the needs of students in their classrooms, allowing them to make adjustments based on specific knowledge about specific learners. We don't do much of this any more

We've come a long way since then, and have moved from helping students and teachers to helping administrators and politicians. Today, standardized tests are principally used to measure people in groups— students, teachers, schools, and others. The results are viewed competitively, comparing classrooms, schools, districts, states, or even countries, with one another, pressuring educators and schools to improve poor performance.

Of course, this is intended to improve education. But improvement comes one student at a time, by attending to the needs of every learner, top to bottom. Standardized tests are powerful instruments which could identify these needs, and help teachers deal better with individual students.

We sacrifice this on the altar of decision-making by public officials. This is by not, I repeat, not the best use of standardized testing.

We should be able to use the details of a student's performance to identify where he or she needs help. This cannot be done if protecting an instrument's security limits its public inspection. So, a teaching opportunity is lost. I might add that some efforts are now being made to provide more information about student performance, although not about individuals. Schools simply are told which areas need work.

Critics say that using tests to compare teachers, schools, or other groups impedes education by forcing instructors to "teach for the test." This can mean anything from telling students what the test will be like, to spending class time on the areas it will emphasize, to giving practice exams. If any of this occurs, the test has to that extent become the master of the curriculum, and its areas of focus will be those of the school, regardless of what any local syllabus might say.

Critics have also called attention to the stresses involved. The knowledge that it's intended to evaluate the teacher or the school, or both, can make students nervous about this somewhat exotic activity. Not to say that it doesn't also make at least some teachers nervous. They've even been known to spend class time on test-taking strategies—a dubious practice at best.

The time required to explain the test's necessity, provide preparation for it, and administer it, is time not devoted to the regular curriculum. So the use of major testing programs is a mixed bag. I'm not saying present practice is undesirable. I do say the results come at a cost.

When we use a test this way, we should do so with caution. We should note how it influences instruction, and how much it reduces time given to areas desired by the district, or to other desirable activities. We should compare its scope and emphasis to those of the curriculum. We must take care not to allow it to acquire a life of its own.

What teachers can do. Not much, if you're thinking of a state-wide or district-wide testing program. This is a fact of life today, and all one can do is face it realistically, and try to keep it from distorting the curriculum and classroom too much.

But there's much teachers can do about their own practices. Although improvement is complicated by their lack of knowledge about test construction and analysis, as well as their conviction that subject-matter mastery assures mastery of evaluation. Still, I'll try to be helpful.

1. Any test you create should be valid. It should match the contents of the course. The simplest way to do this is to make sure every piece of information, every procedure, every understanding in the test was actually dealt with in the classroom, and had as important a place there as it does in the test. Anything dealt with only orally, or in footnotes, should not be used.

2. The test should be reliable, too. This is hard to ensure. At the very least, it needs all language to be unambiguous, and objective questions should not give unconscious clues or represent a mix of your language and that of a book. A test should contain items of at least three levels of difficulty. Probably, another teacher, or a supervisor, should be asked to read it, to see if changes are needed.

3. Avoid scouring the textbook, or other materials, looking for obscure matters to use. Generally speaking, esoteric information is a poor way to make a test harder, since it focuses on memory more than understanding.

4. Try using an open-book exam. Since any question asking for simple facts can be answered by simply reading, you're forced to ask questions dealing with understandings. What the student remembers can be measured at anther time in a different test.

5. Create a file of questions which have been used, noting their date of use, and the percentage of correct answers. In a short time, this will result in a collection which can be drawn upon for future exams. Because of the effort involved, items should be preserved and protected for future use, and should be improved regularly.

6. Tests should not be used solely to determine a student's level of achievement. More important is analysis of answers, to locate the test-taker's areas of strength and weakness—especially helpful for planning remedial work.

7. I don't recommend doing extensive item analysis, although that's the best way to demonstrate reliability. It's difficult, time-consuming, and requires special training or coursework. I'll limit my suggestions to those above.

8. If an outside testing program is used, stick to suggested procedures to the letter. Use authorized materials only, and don't make more, or different, preparatory efforts than are recommended. Especially, don't spend class time on test-taking strategies. Not only does this divert class time from relevant learning, it may skew results, and is unprofessional.

9. Examine all standardized tests used, if possible, to see how closely their content matches that of the syllabus or curriculum. Since school authorities are concerned too, they should welcome your calling attention to any discrepancies.

10. Since the best use of standardized tests is to diagnose students' needs, try to get some breakdown of students' performance on various areas of the test, even anonymously. Ask if such information is available. If you can get discarded tests, use them for diagnosis.

What principals and supervisors can do. Certainly, they should be as helpful as possible to all teachers seeking to improve their testing procedures. They also have the responsibility for maintaining the integrity and ensuring the proper administration of any standardized tests used.

Everything I've said earlier about helping teachers change is valid here. I'll make some specific suggestions.

1. Provide all the help you can—materials, consultants, course work— for any teacher asking for assistance in test construction.

2. Consider focusing an in-service program on the creation and proper use of tests.

3. Encourage teachers in the same field to share ideas and coordinate test construction and usage.

4. Share all thoughtful comments by teachers about any standardized test with higher administration.

5. Make an effort to obtain any information you can about test results which could help teachers identify students' needs

6. Make certain that teachers administer standardized tests correctly, and are familiar with the proper ways of preparing students for them.

What parents can do. Parents should be concerned when tests are used to assess their school's excellence, since major change can occur if performance is poor. They have a right to know what's being done, and why.

So far as testing by teachers is concerned, they have a right to an explanation if their child experiences fear or anxiety, or complains of unfairness. They should helped to feel confident that testing is done fairly and competently.

Here's what I think a parent can do.

1. If a test score surprises and disappoints, find out what happened, and discuss with the teacher what your child can do to improve. Try to help the child understand and accept.

2. If your child complains of unfairness, or shows fear or anxiety about a test, talk to the teacher and try to agree on how you both will approach the problem.

3. Discuss with the teacher any negative factors in the child's reactions to the testing regularly done in the classroom.

4. Inform yourself about any standardized testing program being used or proposed—its purpose, what's involved for students, and the school's current level of performance.

5. Talk to your child about any such program, and ascertain any worries or apprehensions. Give him or her factual information about the test's purposes and procedures, and make sure your child knows that no grade will be affected, and the result will not be part of his or her record.

PART THREE

The Challenge of Change

N OW THAT WE'VE GOT TESTING, GRADING, READING, HOMEWORK, and "telling" settled (hooray!), it's time to look at other matters. And there are others, believe it or not.

Seriously, I propose that we reexamine almost all educational practices, not because they're defective (although I do believe many of them are), but because in my opinion every major endeavor in life should be questioned from time to time. We should see if their assumptions are still valid and they still fulfill the purposes for which they were originally created.

Society has changed vastly since the American public school system was instituted. Many new challenges face us, and we have gained many new insights. Have the objectives of education changed, and is it achieving them?

This is a major undertaking, and I don't pretend to do more than scratch the surface. But I'll describe in this Part Three how the scratching might be done, and in Part Four, what needs scratching.

To be a little more informative, I'm going to review the best professional thinking, as I understand it, on how to plan and evaluate an educational program. I'll describe the conditions within which planning must be done and the factors that influence it. Then, I'll consider the need to identify outcomes, how to develop experimental efforts, and how to assess results.

Part Four will contain a discussion of those features of education we need to look at anew. Specifically, I'll suggest practices and questions worth study and experimentation.

7. Moving the Queen Mary

So far, I've focused on what can be done within the existing educational system. Scattered here and there, I may have implied a need for major change, usually when I was trying to justify something to do in the here-and-now. But here-and-now is not good enough. We need major change, and I do mean major, if education is to be all ~~that~~ it might be.

But getting such change is like towing the Queen Mary with a rowboat. Not only do you have the massive weight of the monster, but there are also its many ties to the pier. In schools, the boat is the totality of the system and the ties are impediments to change.

It's foolish to think a little book like this one can be even a strong swimmer, let alone a rowboat. But I'm determined to say my piece, since I'm convinced things need revision. If I can persuade even one person of this, I'll be glad.

Many school practices are hoary with age, and bear an uncomfortable resemblance to what I saw as a child eighty-plus years ago. Many of those practices have almost never been questioned. Some may have served a purpose at one time, but don't do so today. Isn't it defeatist to do what's always been done, without requiring occasional re-justification or some rethinking?

I don't mean to say that everything is unchanged. We've added courses to the curriculum, removed desks screwed to the floor, and now have counselors and nurses. Opportunities for the handicapped are mandated by law. Blackboards are mostly gone and school buses have mostly arrived. Specialized training for administrators was not around in 1925, and the N.E.A. was a professional organization which included school administrators and college professors.

Much curricular change has occurred over the years. Latin has lost ground, industrial arts and home economics (under many different names) have gained. But the more recently an area has appeared, the more it's under pressure if financial straits occur. Look at driver education, art, music, home ec, industrial arts, foreign languages, even P.E.—all have been under the gun somewhere at some time. But people rarely question math or physics or English.

I don't say these so-called solid subjects are of doubtful value. But I do say we should look at them afresh, identify the benefits they have for later life, and whether they benefit all students alike. We should also review the appropriate ages for their introduction. We shouldn't assume we already know the answers. We might find that some of our "knowledge" is not that at all.

The schools are a living organism which must adapt to changing circumstances, and be reassessed from time to time. I'm well aware that this is a huge undertaking. But not doing it allows tradition and lethargy to replace evidence.

Modifying education is a lot more than influencing teachers. Our schools represent a massive and complex structure, and changing it requires the consensus of the citizenry. Deep-rooted practices and conditions change only with widespread support. And how does this support come about? It requires information, communication, persuasion, and conviction. Most of all it's a matter of spreading the word when something works.

How do we do that?

The broken-front approach. Even when an idea is good or a practice is proven to be effective, how is it possible to persuade everyone everywhere, or even get information to many people in many places? Our methods of mass communication fall short of universal coverage, unless an event is dramatic or tragic to an extreme. Yet major educational change must be grounded on widespread changes of opinion.

I think the only hope for doing this is what is called the broken-front approach. This odd name reflects the strength of a system in which every school is locally controlled, and the federal, or even the state, government is limited in its power to coerce or influence. There are thousands of school districts in the nation, and each is empowered to make its own decisions. Although education is legally under state control, authority has been largely ceded to local school boards, usually with some state-wide conditions. Yet, an amazing feature of this system is how much similarity there is across the country.

I once had an official from the Iceland Ministry of Education ask me how we could tolerate so many people making independent decisions. He asked, "How can you be sure necessary actions are taken?" I asked him in exchange how he could be sure his department always knew the best things for every school to do. No single group of individuals can ever conceive of all the possibilities which can occur to people in the thousands, or be knowledgeable about all the conditions they face.

This is the essence of the broken-front approach. With a multitude of minds at work, many new ideas see the light of day. And word of successful efforts gets around. This is the best way we've found to distribute information and evidence. And it's possible only because of local control.

The widespread similarity in programs and practices grows out of widespread consensus. We see agreement among citizens generally, and educators particularly. The challenge facing all innovators is how to generate this.

Any new proposal needs to be adopted by only a handful of schools to be given a chance. And there are always localities willing to try promising ideas. Word gets out if an experiment works well. People come to observe, and the practice spreads. If we had to wait for a centralized department of education to suggest change, we'd wait a long time, and see fewer proposals.

This is the broken-front approach—with thousands of school districts and countless experiments ever present . The arrangement leads to more and better change than any centralized system.

If you need further evidence, think of a super-sized school district, like New York City. With innumerable schools, varying needs of neighborhoods, huge numbers of people to influence, immense difficulties of communication and coordination, as well as the politics endemic to a large organization, how can change be managed from the center? And how can it not be? Big-city districts which do the best, though, are those allowing schools some degree of autonomy.

The broken-front approach attacks the problem of gaining consensus. Innovations are reported in newspapers and journals, witnessed by visitors, and discussed at conferences. Studies with good results are tried elsewhere. Thus we have information, communication, persuasion, and eventually, conviction. It takes time of course, much time, but this is the way to consensus. This is how to move the Queen Mary.

Now, I'll look at its land connections—the barriers and impediments to change. What are these and what do we do about them?

8. The conditions which prevail.

Educational change occurs in a setting where a myriad of forces are at work. I'll describe these and how they might affect the task. The first is the maelstrom of emotions which are ever present. Later, I'll delineate other factors with which we have to contend.

The maelstrom of emotions. If a school wants to do anything that threatens serious change, it generates a world of strong feelings— axes to grind, turf to defend, fears and anxieties, demands of parents and others, convictions pro and con, ambition and competition, you name it. Everyone wants to get into the act, even if only to oppose what's proposed.

If the change would have a widespread impact, the community gets involved. (It may anyway.) Politicians orate. Government requirements are invoked. Unions take stands. School boards issue directives. Professors deplore the preparation of freshmen. We've got it all.

This is the mix within which school planners must plan, authorities must make decisions, and teachers must work. Teachers especially are often at a loss to know how to avoid displeasing people without compromising their beliefs and standards.

My first proposal is to cool the inflammatory language. If a district faces too much controversy, it should establish a forum to do several things: 1) provide factual information about current practices and results, 2) identify issues, and report the best thinking on all sides, 3) prioritize, to ensure that not everything is argued at once, and 4) establish procedures for cool-headed discussion.

Such a forum should represent all interested parties, especially the parents. But if it's composed of respected persons, and charged with achieving the above elements, there's a fighting chance fiery issues can be resolved calmly.

The more a particular idea is innovative, though, and especially if it brings into question any of the sacred cows of education or the moral or religious convictions of people, the more care is needed No new project should be undertaken unless and until there's widespread support for the basic idea.

The only hope, then, in an emotional maelstrom is cooperative planning, with everyone involved, everyone having a chance to be heard, and everyone's opinions being given serious consideration. And it all must be done without angry, inflammatory, or accusatory language.

All these breezy comments—do this, do that, change this, evaluate that—make it sound easy. I know it's not. In fact, it's horrendously hard. It requires adept leadership if all parties are to feel valued. There's much work, too—getting data, looking at other programs, soliciting the help of consultants, and preparing materials.

We know thoughtful people can disagree. We also know that democracy requires compromise (even if Congress doesn't seem to). We've found that when passions cool, and everyone feels heard, most people accept what the majority decides. I'm optimistic about reaching this outcome under the right conditions.

I'll not suggest a specific structure for organizing the job. We already have faculty meetings, teacher-parent conferences, PTA sessions. We have teacher evaluation, in-service programs, school board meetings, and other regular or irregular contacts. What counts is true involvement, regardless of the form it takes. What's essential is openness.

9. The tie-downs

I use the term, tie-downs, in accord with my earlier image of a rowboat towing a liner. These are the factors, either immutable or at least extremely strong, which can be stumbling blocks for planners, who can trip on them and fail to recover.

Impediments come in various forms. One is the resistance which is almost endemic to humankind. Add the expectations of the community, including the parents (especially the parents), as well as those of colleges and employers. Then, there are aspects of reality, like finances and laws and teacher tenure. Finally, many special-interest groups exist, most notably teachers' organizations, often with passionate adherents and strongly-held positions. I'll consider them in turn.

Resistance. This is the face of much of the emotional maelstrom I've just described. And it's everywhere. Teachers worry about not being able to learn new practices. Subject specialists fear for their special areas of interest. Parents are afraid their children won't go to a "good" college or get a good job. Citizens are reluctant to raise taxes. It's basic for humans to cling to the familiar and comfortable, and not want to go into the cold of the new and different.

Resistance can range from simple dislike of change, to security with old ways and insecurity with new ones, to implacable determination. Dread of failure can be overwhelming at times. Innovators have the challenge of dispelling resistance.

How should this challenge be faced? Many methods have been tried, including coercion, rewards, persuasion, leading the way, demonstration, and various psychological approaches. Often, they don't succeed.

I've already discussed this earlier, both when I suggested how principals and supervisors might influence teacher change and when I considered how to make sense out of a whirlpool of factors. I've said that true change comes only from within, and then only after a person gains new insights. The task, then, is finding ways to help people do that.

I first learned this in a course on mental health when I was already in my thirties. It was then that I saw that curriculum workers and supervisors had the same challenge as psychotherapists and counselors. They all seek to help people change, and must face the fact that telling them directly doesn't work.

For whatever reason, asking someone straight out to do something different, even in a supportive, non-critical, factual manner, often serves to arouse stubbornness. We must emulate the methods of psychotherapists, who face this challenge with every patient. Only then, can we hope change might occur.

I hear you ask, "How can this be done by persons without special training?" I'll try to be helpful. One way is providing opportunities to watch others who are achieving success. This is where the broken front comes in. And it works best when they observe on their own initiative. Providing information about what's going on in various places is a good thing to do. For instance, a committee can canvass ongoing efforts, and summarize its findings, pro and con.

Another thought is that if someone in a school is trying something new, or inquiring about it, the principal or supervisor should be as supportive as possible, without pushing—admiring the effort, offering to help—but taking no for an answer if resistance arises. A facilitator wants to maximize every teacher's chances of success, but it won't happen if criticism is even implied. This is terribly hard to avoid when presenting something new. It's easy to doom efforts from the start.

Every educational leader has to find his or her own way. But it must involve participation by everyone, open discussion, and freewill efforts to reach consensus.

This approach is essential in the educational family, with its considerable mutual respect and trust. It's even more vital in the community, where deeply-held, often clashing, convictions guarantee resistance to almost any suggestion. Many of the impediments I've listed seem to radiate resistance—teachers unions, parental expectations, strong convictions, subject-matter associations. Even with the involvement of all serious factions, the chance of dissension and continued resistance is very high. Educators must be very careful.

Evaluation is a major key. If people have evidence that something works, it may help allay anxieties. And assurance that assessment is built into a proposal may give confidence that things can't go far wrong. Evaluation should be part of every experiment at every stage of its operation, and not just at the finish.

I'll discuss evaluation in more detail later. For now, I'll simply say that without it, the chance of people accepting the challenge of change is remote.

Expectations. What do I mean by expectations? Don't we deal with these when we consider goals and objectives? Whose expectations are we talking about? And what are they? How can they be an impediment? Isn't it the school's job to fulfill the expectations of the citizenry—our bosses?

Everyone has expectations, the man on the street, parents (especially), colleges, employers, everyone. And they all differ, at least to some extent. The expectations of the community are central to the schools and to any proposal for change. So are those of parents, who are of course part of the community. And with their children in school, parents' contact with educators is immediate, and they have the most to gain or lose. Differences among expectations present a challenge, and can be a barrier to change.

The first thing to remember, though, is that the schools should do what the community wants. The board is charged with that responsibility. I'm not sure, though, what the man on the street would say if asked what his expectations are. He might feel strongly about costs or standards, student behavior, personal values, or some special subject-field. But unless he's a parent of a present or former school kid, or has had recent contact with education, he might say something vaguely general, like " Do a good job of preparing students for life" (or for college, or for work, or whatever).

Of all expectations, those of parents are perhaps the most dominant, often based on college expectations, or at least on how these are perceived. Parents form an active and determined group, with many convinced that preparation for higher education is the most critical part of the schools' responsibility. And how can we say otherwise? Students who go to college surely include many of tomorrow's leaders. Their education is vital.

These parents often demand, and I do mean, demand, that the schools prepare their children for college. They often believe this compels the high school to offer the so-called solid subjects. And parents convinced that a prestigious institution is the answer to their aspirations can be the most demanding of all.

I once had a mother of this stripe bend my ear for an hour at a party, complaining because her daughter's high school had dropped its course on Shakespeare, and asking me to what she could do about it. When I asked why she thought such a specialized class was valuable, she said it was something everyone should take. When I further asked how many took it the last time it was taught, she answered, "Three."

What about other parents? What expectations do they have? Possibly, their main desire is for the schools to prepare their children for the world of work. How do we resolve conflict among parental expectations?

How do we handle the wishes of colleges and employers? There's little doubt that the former have long dominated school programs, and any proposal for change must face the inertia of the past. But college expectations seem to have changed over the years, and I don't think we've taken this into account as well as we should have.

As for employers, we haven't done a good job of asking them what they want and need. Their criteria are apparently not as vocational as you might think. Mainly, they seem to look for a well-balanced individual who can learn on the job, and think constructively and creatively. This includes the ability to speak and write correct English, get along with others, and be a conscientious worker. Maybe the colleges want these outcomes too, since, according to their statements, they value well-rounded individuals. And their graduates will eventually enter the world of work.

We face all these factors when we undertake to make change in education. So we need knowledgeable participation, and as wide a consensus as possible. We must serve all groups without letting one any one dominate.

Finances. As an impediment to change, finances are a different set of dishes from resistance and expectations. These latter are human factors which may be influenced by adroit efforts. But the amount of money available is a fact of life, often decreed by voters and administrators. It's conceivable that their decisions might be influenced, but any effort to do so is beyond the focus of this book.

Probably, more proposals for change are aborted because money is unavailable than for any other reason. Shortage of funds is endemic in education and seems everlasting as well. I'm no expert on school finance, but I do have some things to say. I hope you find them reasonable and useful.

We expect a lot for our education dollar. If you divide the average amount spent annually per student by a 180-day school year and a 30-hour school week, the resulting figure approximates what parents spend for an hour of baby sitting. For this we get counseling and various other services, extracurricular activities, athletic and other entertainment, transportation, in addition to teaching. Nonetheless, many people feel they pay too much, and criticize the schools for wanting more.

Part of the controversy is that there's little evidence that more money results in better education. Budget increases are not always, or even often, accompanied by changes in student performance. And many smaller and poorer school districts have done better than others with bigger budgets.

Nevertheless, wealthier areas generally have better results than poorer ones. Schools are financed through local property taxes, and if the property valuation per student is higher in one place than another, the former will have more to spend. The state tries to offset this discrepancy by providing extra funds to poorer districts, but rarely does it compensate. A fact of life is that some children have more spent on them than others.

And since there's no real agreement on how dollars affect outcomes, almost any proposal calling for extra financial support is controversial. It's not so much that citizens are unwilling to spend money on their children, it's that they don't want to spend it unless they're convinced it will improve matters. Any proposal must provide convincing evidence, and include an effective plan for measuring its success.

There's also another issue concerning educational finance. It's the difficulty of comparing present outlays with future ones. For example, all suggestions to salvage young people who are at risk of dropping out of school require funding. Yet, dropouts eventually cost society dearly, through welfare, medical expenses, drug addiction, and delinquency. These later outlays are almost certainly greater than any school effort would be. But no one is certain, and no one has calculated with any certainty the amount of either.

Furthermore, different agencies are involved. Educational costs affect school districts, while any savings for prisons, hospitals, or welfare benefit other branches of government. And the reverse is also true. If school limits on spending result in young people dropping out, the eventual cost will be borne by the Department of Corrections, or other bodies.

Perhaps the government or some foundation will underwrite a longitudinal study of a representative urban school district, to find out how much the cost to salvage, say, fifty percent of the dropout population, compares with future outlays for that same group. The study should also consider any increase in tax revenues if more persons are employed or have better jobs. I think such a study would find that earlier costs would more than pay for themselves through later gains.

I have no idea how to solve the problem of gains and losses at different times in separate agencies. But it certainly makes sense to compare present expenses with future ones. ("Pay me now, or pay me later," as the automobile oil commercial suggests.) Every agency involved is a branch of government, and all are under the control of elected leaders. We are an intelligent nation, and should be able to resolve a difficulty, once it's been identified.

To get back to proposals for change, however, each has to be examined on a cost-benefit basis, and this will always be subjective. No one can be absolutely sure a proposal will work, and no one can know for certain that the result will justify the expenditure. Costs must be carefully calculated and benefits carefully described, together with a plan for assessing results. This way, both the community and school board will have a basis for decision. But if projections and estimates made in earlier projects have turned out to be realistic, confidence in a new analysis will be increased. Once again, evaluation is vital

Sometimes a proposal, like turning a class into a study session or using more volunteers, might even save money. This doesn't happen often, but if it does, finance is no longer a problem.

Laws. These are another fact of life. And again I'll have nothing to say about how they might be changed. Probably, the reader already knows far more than I do. As voters who elect state legislatures, we're all inundated with passionate appeals, seeking our support for or against some law or another. But I do have something to say about laws regarding education.

These range from school finance, to teacher certification and tenure, to standardized testing, to almost anything attracting the attention of politicians. Legislators may give priority to certain activities, such as special programs for the handicapped, or mandate specific subjects, like state history. Voters may also make laws through initiative or referendum. And school boards issue mandates, which are tantamount to legislation so far as any school or teacher is concerned.

Among the more controversial laws are those dealing with teacher tenure. Many people consider tenure to be a hindrance to the schools' moving forward, although many consider it a strength. Since I want to deal with it at length, and it's such a part of teachers' rights and responsibilities, I'll include it in the next section.

Anyone wishing to innovate may be constricted by laws, or forced to give priority to some specified area. If this is the case, so be it. Such mandates reflect society's wishes, and educators are servants of society. They should do the best they can, but if allowable, should prioritize among the various mandates. Since these usually represent important areas, anything done is worthwhile. We should think of them as instructions to be followed rather than impediments to change.

Sometimes, circumstances are warped by laws. For instance, Colorado voters recently adopted a constitutional amendment mandating an annual increase in state-level financial support for public schools. When the recession set in, this area continued to increase rather than contract, a fact which was widely viewed as the cause of a sharp reduction in funds for higher education. Another example is any national mandate for special treatment of a special group which doesn't provide sufficient funds for its implementation.

All citizens should be aware that legislation requiring any specific educational program or emphasis may have unintended side effects. They should inform themselves of any such circumstances, and if convinced they're undesirable, should actively seek change.

Finally, I want to speak about federal laws affecting the schools. Since the U.S. constitution makes no mention of education, Washington has no direct control. But there are two major ways in which the federal government exerts influence. One is giving money; the other is requiring equal treatment of minorities and persons with special needs.

I'll not review the struggle of minorities and others to gain equal footing in education. This story is well known. But I will talk about federal aid, which often has widespread local effects. By giving funds to states, districts, or schools willing to focus on areas of interest to Congress and the Department of Education, federal funds have affected local priorities. "No Child Left Behind" and "Race to the Top" are recent examples. But, there have been many other efforts.

There's been controversy about them, though. Local control of education is an essential part of the American scene, and critics of federal aid say it results in an ever-increasing creep toward centralization. I take no position on this, but urge you to familiarize yourself with federal activities, and decide what you believe.

For purposes of this discussion, though, I'll treat federal assistance very much as I do all laws and mandates. It stresses certain areas in preference to others, and is another fact of life. If it supports an endeavor in which teachers are interested, it might well be a source of funds. They should inform themselves about activities receiving such support, and if any are important to them, should make application. This involves creating a lengthy proposal adhering to extensive guidelines produced by the Department of Education, which must be followed precisely.

In my opinion, it's worthwhile to do this. If a match is located, something might get funded which would perish under local strictures. Further, the preparation of a grant proposal itself represents a learning experience for everyone involved, may influence their ideas, and improve their relations with one another.

In summary, laws are a fact of life, and as such, may influence decisions on what innovations to undertake.

Teachers' organizations. I shouldn't call these an impediment to change, but, rather, an influence on it. There's no doubt that they are that.

The largest and best known of these bodies is the National Education Association (N.E.A.), created over a century ago to gather together **all** concerned educators—teachers, administrators, college professors, and specialists. It has come a long way since then. Teachers took it over, ousted administrators, and turned it into a force for their own rights. Today, it's widely considered to be a union.

There's another union, the American Federation of Teachers (A.F.T.), which is affiliated with the AFL-CIO, and is frankly just that, a union. Both the N.E.A. and the A.F.T. are concerned with any educational change which affects teachers, and many large school districts have personnel mainly concerned with negotiating with them.

Of course, unions exist to foster and protect their members' rights, and anything new that teachers are asked to do is looked at from this perspective. School districts are well aware of this, and make certain that union representation is involved in most proposals for change. Indeed, such activity is almost a daily occurrence for some

At this point, I must confess that I'm a member of the National Educational Association, somewhat to my bemusement. When I was a young professor, the N.E.A. was still very much under the influence of school administrators and college professors. At that time, I took advantage of a special offer, and paid a lump sum for a life membership.

Over time, it gradually changed into the force you see today. For years, though, it sent me its publications, which I found of increasingly less interest. Still, it intrigued me to be a member, since I don't believe in the unionization of education. It also amused me when, about ten years ago, mailings to me ceased. Someone must have decided I was dead, or at least should be. So much for life membership.

I'll start this discussion positively. Without a doubt, unionization has led to teachers having more impact on educational decisions, including curricular ones, than they used to have. At one time, their opinions were rarely solicited or welcomed. Also beyond a doubt, working conditions have improved, salaries have increased, and wage scales now exist nearly everywhere.

On the other hand, unions have been known to block curricular change, and there have been strikes. I hate teachers' strikes, even though I know why they occur, and have often agreed with the teachers' position.

I feel, though, that there's something contradictory in a strike by teachers. The same persons, the vast majority of whom I'm convinced care deeply for their students, are the ones who create a hindrance to children's education. I know the justification is advanced that the strike will benefit them in the long run, but I'm not always so sure. I keep feeling there are better ways to settle issues, and we must find them.

Teachers control their unions, but that's not to say they always exercise their power. On major matters, the majority rules. But many issues are not seen as sufficiently major to bring to the membership. They're left to union executives, who may not have the same priorities as members.

These executives typically see the union as their first order of business, and consider teachers' wages, rights, benefits, and well-being their number-one priority. In consequence, they may view proposed changes primarily in terms of how they impact such matters. and secondarily on how they might affect students and parents. But most union leaders are educators too and, at heart, care for children. Still, they have a point of view, and unless this is taken seriously innovation can run into trouble. Unions certainly are an influence on change, and in some circumstances, can be an impediment to it.

Besides these organizations, there are innumerable others—specialists in specific subject fields, or teachers involved in special programs like teaching the handicapped, or persons who perform a school function, like principals, supervisors, or counselors. Such groups exist primarily to share ideas, and improve matters within their areas of concern. If they become involved in a school's effort to innovate, they typically do so in a supplementary role. Usually, they attempt to influence educational change through printed materials or public statements.

Dealing with special-interest groups requires the kind of cooperative planning I've already discussed. The union is likely to be the one which receives most attention. Its number-one focus being on teacher welfare, it may feel that effort making curricular or instructional changes might affect it negatively.

For example, union opposition to merit pay and evaluation of instruction, and its steadfast support of teacher tenure, can constitute a potential impediment. Still, many districts have gained union agreement to an experiment once it felt safeguards were in place. After all, if all interested parties are involved, some are bound to be union members or officials.

I've already said that all proposals need to include an assessment plan. This must involve judging teachers' effectiveness properly. If plans have been made cooperatively, with due regard for teacher input, it should not endanger their rights. This might disarm resistance, unless prior local conflict about tenure or merit pay has resulted in major resistance.

Tenure. At this point, I must consider teacher tenure—one of the more controversial areas in today's educational world. This protection is much debated, much criticized, and is a major concern of unions. It's closely associated with such issues as evaluation of instruction and merit pay. And it intermingles with teacher education and certification, about which I shall say more later. Needless to say, teachers' unions are advocates of tenure, and resistant to any proposal which threatens it.

Their resistance is deep-seated. And their leaders have a vested self-interest in protecting dues-paying members. If any change is to occur in the tenure system, if can happen only if union concerns can be dealt with, and certainly only if an effective approach to evaluation can be found—one with widespread acceptability.

So what is tenure? Contrary to widespread belief, it's not a career-long guarantee of a job. Rather, it specifies by law strict requirements for dismissing tenured personnel, and mandates that due process be used. In practice, however, the procedures necessary to secure a dismissal are arduous and time-consuming, with considerable difficulty in gathering convincing evidence. As a result, it's seldom done, and many poor teachers are allowed to continue teaching, thus giving the impression of lifelong job security.

It came about originally, very much like civil service, from a need to protect a system from abuse. Before its appearance, teachers could be told what to teach or not teach, regardless of their convictions. A bigoted, overbearing, or ignorant principal might compel conformity or impose onerous conditions under the threat of discharge. Also, penny-pinching school boards might try to save money by replacing all their experienced (and higher paid) faculty with beginners.

Over the years, though, tenure has morphed into a subject of controversy. There's no doubt that it has shielded many incompetents from dismissal. Yet, if that were made easier, the abuses it's designed to prevent might reappear. It's a catch-twenty-two situation—damned if you do, damned if you don't.

Critics say we've gone too far, and dismissal of incompetent instructors should be made easier. Also, they suggest that tenure be harder to attain in the first place. Many propose that it be for a fixed term of years, with review at that time. These and other suggestions for amending the system abound.

Supporters remind us of the original reasons for tenure, and see its value as outweighing its defects. But many of them seem open to suggestions for improvement, while insisting that its basic purposes not be breached. Yet teachers fear that evaluation will be done unfairly or incompetently, or that self-serving individuals might "game" the system. Still, in my lifetime. I've found most teachers to be conscientious, professional, and reasonable. Many would be open to a properly conducted evaluation program. They just have to be sure it's done right.

The question is how to do it right. It requires a valid and reliable procedure, conducted with objectivity and competence, and avoidance of a negative emotional impact which might damage a teacher's effectiveness. A way must be found to do all this dependably and professionally.

There's no doubt that an instructor's effectiveness is critical to good education. Many persons outside the profession see no reason why it shouldn't be a simple matter to judge this by how students do on achievement tests. And when they hear a plethora of reasons-why-not, they assume this is simply defensiveness on the part of educators, who seem to them to be circling the wagons.

But using students' performance founders on several counts. Since classes vary in ability, some variation in achievement is normal. And any learning acquired before a class begins can skew results. In addition, class size and availability of resources can impact a teacher's effectiveness.

Making use of student test-results could work *IF* 1) there's absolute confidence in the quality of the test, 2) there's a close match between its focus and that of the curriculum, 3) students' level of achievement is determined at the time they enter the teacher's classroom, so that only the progress they make since then can be attributed to that teacher, and 4) the test is properly administered. All these are challenging, but doable.

But even if worthwhile information is obtained this way, it reveals only the subject-matter effectiveness of the teacher. It says little about his or her influence on students' work habits, assiduousness, ability to think critically, social skills, moral values, or love of learning. Such information is particularly hard to determine, yet many such outcomes figure prominently in statements of educational objectives.

Nor does it say anything about a teacher's counseling skills, effectiveness with parents, or performance in cooperative faculty responsibilities. I don't presume to say that all the foregoing should be part of an evaluation program, but I do say that whenever any of it is included, it present a considerable extra challenge. In brief, judging teacher effectiveness by looking solely at students' classroom achievement, is at best just a piece of the task.

Then, there's the issue of who should do the evaluating and how that person can be found. At present, there's little evidence that principals or supervisors are uniquely qualified, since many individuals are appointed to leadership positions for reasons other than classroom effectiveness. We often see administrators whose efforts at evaluating instruction are not viewed by faculty members as fair and reasonable. And as for teachers assessing the work of their peers, this approach generally not achieved promising results.

But the community seems to want teachers' job security and level of pay to be based upon a measure of their effectiveness. There's widespread support for merit pay. Isn't this the essence of a free economic system? Shouldn't teachers be subjected to the same process everyone else has to face? All that's needed is an effective way to evaluate teacher competence.

But there's the rub. It's so complex, so difficult, so subjective. Still. much experimentation is going on, although achieving consensus is difficult, with so much mistrust among groups. The problem is that everyone's right. Incompetents are sometimes protected, judgments are often questionable and/or damaging, and much valuable information is elusive.

My conclusion is to recommend that evaluation of instruction receive special attention. All interested parties must seek agreement on what elements to include, and an earnest effort be made to find or create appropriate instruments. It is also critical to develop criteria and procedures for finding qualified individuals who can do the evaluation professionally and competently. Ideally, such persons should not be the ones responsible for hiring-and-firing decisions.

Without a doubt, effective evaluation of teachers is crucial for the success of our schools. If it can be done achieved, incompetents can be weeded out, tenure becomes a non-issue and merit pay will be the standard. But it's easy to say what the schools should do, but frustratingly difficult for them to accomplish in the real world. I shall have more to say about tenure when I consider standards of the educational profession in Part Five.

PART FOUR

The Process of Change

N OW I'LL LOOK AT HOW ANY SERIOUS EFFORT TO CHANGE SHOULD BE produced and conducted. The process should never be undertaken casually, especially if it questions something long established. There should be reasoning behind it, it should have supporting evidence, it should accord with the experience and beliefs of those involved, and it should be meticulously prepared. It will stress evaluation, and involve parents and all teachers affected. I assume it will be consistent with the principles of good schooling presented earlier in this book.

And where does change come from? There's the board of education, and possibly an advisory committee. There's the school superintendent, principals, supervisors, and faculties. To say nothing of parents, the community, and outside influences. The answer is that a good idea can come from anyone. Sometimes, an administrative proposal catches on. Perhaps the work of a single teacher inspires others. Achievements elsewhere may spark a desire to emulate. An idea can appear anywhere, and if it shines, can make a great difference.

School districts should encourage experimentation with promising new ideas, and be open to everyone's suggestions. This is not to say that every random thought is worth pursuing, although it might stimulate brainstorming, and lead to better ideas. It *is* to say that worthwhile change emerges from creative thinking, and this should be welcomed.

The following represents my understanding of the profession's consensus on how a project should be planned and conducted responsibly and competently. I assume any educators undertaking an experimental endeavor know this already, through their training, in-service education, reading of reports, observation of successful efforts, recommendations of experts, and, above all, engaging in widespread participation.

1. Identify goals.

2. Define these in the form of specific objectives.

3. Find or create ways to measure their achievement.

4. Plan and develop procedures for achieving these objectives.

5. Conduct the experimental program.

6. Evaluate results.

I'll describe the challenges presented by each of these, and suggest ways to proceed, focusing on group efforts to improve some important aspect of a school's program or practice.

Although my remarks will be directed mainly toward those working on the endeavor, I intend them to inform all who are interested in improving the schools. I'll try to apply common sense and avoid educational jargon. I hope I have readers who want straight talk.

I'll do my best.

10. Goals and objectives

Many terms are used for what a school aims to accomplish, most notably, purposes, goals, and objectives. These represent a progression from broader to narrower areas of focus. The word, outcomes, is often used also, and it can refer to any of the three.

What does society wants its children to get from their schooling? The answer can be as broad as "be a good citizen" or as narrow as "know who wrote the Declaration of Independence." The former represents a generalized purpose, the latter, a specific objective, in this case, a learning outcome in the social studies. For many, subject-matter achievement is the primary focus of education. For others, a variety of other broad outcomes is also important.

No matter what term is used, it's a nuance of the same concept—what we want to achieve, or rather, what we want our children to achieve. I'll not spend time on a precise definition for any of the terms used since I think developing it would be almost as useless as debating how many angels can dance on the head of a pin. Instead, I'll simply use the word, goals, to refer to broader outcomes of education, and objectives for more specific ones.

Educators and non-educators alike have long obsessed over goals for schools, and where they are to be found. Countless erudite studies have appeared, and many ways to develop them have been suggested.

Long ago, Dr. Ralph Tyler, Director of the Eight-Year Study, proposed that the following areas be examined to obtain goals for education: 1) study of the learner, 2) study of his societal environment, 3) suggestions of subject-matter specialists, 4) a philosophy of education, and 5) the psychology of education. You can see the breadth and depth involved.

Many suggestions are so broad as to be almost useless, and the discussion can get very esoteric. But simultaneously with the over-generalizations, massive lists of specific learnings have been created, mostly by subject-matter specialists. Over the years, countless statements have appeared, including one with which I was involved.

Goals for Education in Colorado. In 1962, when I was at the Colorado Department of Education, I was assigned the task of assisting a committee to prepare a statement of the state's goals for education. Our procedure was to identify major areas, have me prepare draft material for them to read, revise, and eventually adopt.

Needless to say, much of the wording in the final document was language I had prepared. Recently, as I was writing this book, I pulled the ancient document from my files, and reread it. I was shocked by its lack of usefulness. It consisted of eleven goals, stated in such broad terms, and I'm sorry to say, such pompous language, as to be almost without value for teachers or other educators.

I'm still impressed by the care and thought put into it. The goals were worthy, with noble sentiments almost everyone could support, and it received favorable attention at the time. Nevertheless, so far as I know, no school program in the state was altered by it in any way. For your information, I reprint its items. Of course, each was accompanied by several paragraphs of amplification, which I won't include. You can see two things: 1) beautiful generalities don't point to specific action, and 2) not much has changed in 50 years.

1. Command of the knowledge, skills, habits, and attitudes essential for effective learning throughout life.

2. Understanding of man and society, and the determination to strive for the welfare of all people.

3. Knowledge of self, understanding of one's own characteristics and motivations, and appropriate development of individual abilities and interests,

4. Proficiency in recognizing and defining problems, thinking critically, objectively, and creatively about them, and acting constructively toward their solution.

5. Confidence in one's own abilities, courage and initiative in the face of difficulties, and creativity and leadership in resolving them.

6. Skills, attitudes, and understandings necessary for effective group action and satisfying human relationships.

7. Effectiveness in communicating ideas and feelings, and overcoming or avoiding barriers to communication.

8. A philosophy based upon values conducive to sound character, ethical and moral behavior, and democratic action.

9. Wisdom in selecting a lifework, and skills, attitudes, and understandings basic to effectiveness in any lifework.

10. Appreciation of beauty, wherever and however it may be manifested, and the motivation to create it.

11. Knowledge, attitudes, and self-understanding basic to the achievement and maintenance of physical and mental health.

Anyone reading this list can see what's wrong with it. It paints a picture of an almost-perfect human being whom you're not likely to see, especially in the form of a teen-aged youth. It also reveals how hard it would be to apply in any practical way.

To be useful, it would have had to be phrased in language describing something which could be observed readily and with certainty. For instance, what behavior, performance, written material, or creative work would enable you to judge, with reasonable objectivity, the extent to which a student has acquired, say, an appreciation of beauty (item #10)? Even the production of a work of art would not prove the presence of appreciation, especially if the observer has a different definition of beauty than the producer. No statement we produced was in language conducive to objective observation, and all would have needed extensive elaboration to be useful.

I hope I've learned from this experience, and can now produce something which is more helpful, or a least point the way to get there.

Selecting goals. I'll start by trying to organize the clutter of ideas I've seen in a lifetime of work, reading countless statements of educational purpose, many advanced with the greatest passion and urgency. The number of such efforts is unknowable, but it's surely enormous.

However, much of it can be sorted into types, and can be classified according to the following simple list::

Values
Habits
Understandings
Skills
Information

I know this is an extreme oversimplification, and feel almost embarrassed to use it. So much study and thought have been given by so many people whose efforts should be acknowledged and valued. As I've said, the professional literature abounds with proposals. And many schools have developed their own statements, often relying on this wealth of material.

Critics will note many omissions from my list. What about the interests of learners? Or, sensitivity to other people, as well as flexibility and resourcefulness in dealing with them? Or, appreciation of other qualities than beauty? These are attainments which are valued by many people. I'll respond by saying that most such areas can be defined in a way that includes them in one of the headings above.

For example, interests are revealed in the habitual behavior of students, the choices they make, and the things they say. Social sensitivity can be considered a value which a person holds, or the habits he or she displays, or as a body of understandings and skills. Similarly, with honesty, conscientiousness, and good morals.

Consider physical education (mentioned briefly in goal #11), which is both a part of the curriculum and the extra-curriculum. Interscholastic competition can so consume a community that it interferes with calm consideration of other educational needs. Aren't values revealed here? Or understandings, skills, and information? Isn't P.E. presumed to help students, not only to value physical fitness, but to develop habits of good health?

I feel the list is broad enough and flexible enough to encompass almost any outcome I've seen proposed or achieved. It may not be comprehensive, but I think it contains the most important areas. It's just not possible to include all the goals which have been suggested.

Every community must decide what it expects its schools to accomplish, if only to enable educators to develop plans and procedures. As a practical matter, though, creating a set of goals is normally a joint effort, with school personnel providing input based on their familiarity with the issues involved.

Usually, too, they're allowed a certain latitude in setting goals. Only when something offends those with deeply-held convictions does serious controversy arise. Persons with certain religious beliefs, or strong moral positions, may feel their position is endangered. Sometimes, parents can feel the schools are intruding on the family's area of responsibility.

But educators know the areas where citizens feel strongly and where parents bear the prime responsibility, so they steer schools into a supportive role. And careful attention must be paid toward keeping this role supportive. Teachers can be helpful about students' values and habits by reporting observations of their behavior to keep parents informed.

I don't suggest how a school and its community should go about choosing their goals. I'm just saying it should be done. I'll also say that it's very likely that some non-academic ones will appear in the result. I recently read the report of a national survey of mission statements from more than 100 public and private schools of various levels, sizes, and ethnicity. It found more statements dealing with emotional development than with cognitive development. It also revealed a disposition toward highly generalized statements of the kind that appeared in the 1962 document I described above.

What non-academic goals should appear? Again I say this is for the community to decide. I'll discuss in succeeding sections some values and habits which might be considered.

I should note here that many who think subject-matter achievement is the main, if not the only, purpose of education, take the position that anything done about values and habits is of secondary importance. They say subject learning is the reason we have schools in the first place, and areas like the ability to get along with others, should be learned elsewhere. They believe values should be the focus of the family or religious institution, or both, with the school's role one of supporting their efforts, or at least not impeding them. And some people think that acquiring values is mainly the learner's responsibility.

Those who see non-academic outcomes as beyond the school's responsibility have the task of suggesting what should be done about students who cheat or bully, fail to study, or disrupt the class—other than write them off. Others who believe that vague objectives like good learning habits or the ability to do independent thinking are not practical have the responsibility of saying how they think graduates can function without them, or where they'll come from if not from the schools.

However, none of the preceding should be taken to mean that I'm not a supporter of the primacy of academic outcomes. The schools truly exist to pass on the intellectual learnings of the past, and the subject fields are how we do this. I take it as a given that subject-matter achievement is a critical part of every school's goals.

But think of all the fields beyond the solid subjects. Consider art, music, crafts, and home economics. To say nothing about vocational education, such areas as family living, good citizenship, and daily life generally.

Subject fields expect students to gain information, skills, and understandings, although some specialists might also identify relevant habits and values. Nevertheless, many values and habits are outside specific subjects, and closely related to the task of living. If I've spent so much time on such outcomes, it's because they're often a cause of controversy and confusion.

Now that we've discussed educational goals, we face the question of using them. This was the problem we failed to face in Colorado in 1962. We produced an inspirational(?) document, but it was mainly honored in the breach. Much additional work should have been done to make it useful.

What kind of work? How can broad statements of purpose help us decide what to do. and find out how well we did it? We need to translate the language of goals into the language of objectives. These can then direct the planning of programs and activities, and lead to methods of assessment.

Objectives. I've already said that objectives are more specific than goals. And my list of five kinds of outcomes clearly moves from the more general to the more specific.

The challenge for anyone choosing goals is to avoid the over-generalization trap. Broad outcomes must be fleshed out in behavioral terms. Only then will teachers know what to observe as they see students in action. Only when this is done will the schools be assured everyone is working on all educational goals.

Typically, we see the vast majority of specific objectives in the subject fields. And of course, we also see the vast majority of classroom activity, and of evaluation, in these areas. Subject-matter specialists have long since formulated detailed lists of expected learnings. We should become equally adept in doing the same thing for other areas of achievement.

I'll say more about practical issues of specifying objectives, and determining how well they're achieved in a later section. Now I'd like to examine the different kinds of educational outcomes.

Values. I don't believe there's an educator alive who'd disagree with the statement that the family is the main determiner of the moral values a child should acquire and demonstrate, and that helping him or her do that is the parents' job. There's also widespread belief that religious bodies share this responsibility. But the schools also have a legitimate concern with fostering good values.

They have a large stake in this matter. Many situations involve issues of morality. Cheating is one of the most common. Bigotry is another. So is bullying. And moral questions arise when students are mocked for their appearance, handicaps, or immaturity, to say nothing about their ethnicity. The community expects the school to hold high standards in such matters, while not contravening anything that parents do. Educators have a big responsibility, while having to tread carefully

What values should appear in a statement of school purposes? Probably those which are most needed for successful school performance—honesty, consideration for others, respect for rules, cooperation in group-work, at the least. And these are not only necessary for school. They're essential for life outside of school and through the years.

My suggestions are necessarily incomplete. I couldn't begin to formulate a comprehensive list of those I believe in myself, let alone one with which others would agree. This is the task of the community. Still, the school must know what's expected.

Those who endorse values as legitimate goals of education see a vital need for graduates who are thoroughly decent, effective human beings. Almost everyone wants the school system to produce young people who don't lie, or cheat, or act with bigotry. Still, there's much disagreement as to what all this means, and what values are involved. The community wants and needs citizens with good moral habits, whatever they take those to be, and regardless of how active a role they believe the schools should take.

Once there's agreement on what educators should focus on, the question arises of what to do. And it isn't easy. Value statements often fail to influence the curriculum or teachers' activities in any observable way. It is my intention to try to show what can be done.

Habits. Habits are closely related to values. Indeed, they show us the values of the people we see regularly. And we usually place more reliance on actions than words, since many persons don't practice what they preach, "What you do speaks so loud that I cannot hear what you say."

So, the first area of outcomes is connected to this second one. The one represents beliefs that students hold, and the other considers how or if they put them into practice.

Still, statements about habits are often amorphous and ill-defined. For example, what are good study habits? I've seen many guides for teachers' use, without a whole lot of agreement among them. I'm not about to define the term myself, but I shall note that among the various elements I've noticed are the following abilities: to take notes, to discriminate between key ideas and supplementary ones, to organize one's time and materials, to show self-discipline, as well as others. If good study habits are to be made an educational outcome, they need to be carefully defined in detail.

What habits are particularly needed at school? Good work habits is clearly a goal. But what about cooperativeness, or friendliness, or compassion, or simple politeness? Some might call these values, rather than habits. To me, the distinction is meaningless. We believe they're important, regardless of what we call them, and a classroom where any of them is absent would be difficult to manage, and hard to learn in.

Other habits—self-control, using evidence for decision-making, reading for personal satisfaction, a lifelong habit of learning—surely contribute to achievement in the school and are valuable in later life.

Habits are also related to other qualities. Appreciation of music, or literature, or art, or anything, is almost synonymous with the habitual enjoyment of those areas. Interest in a field is reflected similarly. Interests and appreciations appear in many goal statements. But they're usually so generalized as to make them hard to use. They need to be defined behaviorally.

Then too, there are unconstructive habits—smoking, overeating, procrastination, being a couch potato, whatever—which affect our lives. These are a concern to the school when they affect performance there. People who choose the purposes of education should deal with such matters.

Of course, teachers can't act as pseudo-parents, There are limits to how much they can attend to, and there are habits which, although they may affect performance at school, are of greater importance in the home and everyday life.

Deciding which habits are worthy of attention, then, is a challenge. And I'm not being of much help. I've listed some possibilities, but the community will have to decide.

Understandings. Now it gets easier—as I come to the third type of outcome. Understanding is basic to all education, unless we're talking about rote learning. And we've all seen students able to remember lists of presidents and vice-presidents, or states and their capitals, without knowing why they need to know them (by the way, why do they?) Or they can name the countries bordering a nation without knowing how the proximity affects it.

In mathematics, I've seen children memorize the multiplication table, without realizing that multiplication is simply repeated addition, or manipulate algebraic expressions expertly without understanding that algebra is simply arithmetic with unknown numbers.

I remember a third-grade girl who was given the task of calculating the total cost of 15 gallons of gas at $1.80 a gallon (this was some time ago). She said to her teacher, "I can do both addition and multiplication. Which one should I use?"

In any subject, no true learning has taken place until the student knows the meaning and importance of the knowledge which has been acquired, and is able to apply that knowledge effectively in new situations.

Understanding is what makes sense out of facts and skills. It's vital that teachers ensure the information presented in their classes is not just memorized, but is put into meaningful context.

Skills and information. I deal with these two together because they're often combined in class activities, assignments, and tests. Facts and skills are closely interwoven, and for many people, constitute the bulk of the curriculum.

Information is the easiest thing to teach and test for. It's also the most ephemeral learning, readily forgotten unless kept alive through constant use. I believe we spend too much time on the acquisition of information, and should spend more time emphasizing higher forms of learning.

Skills are often first presented as information to be acquired. Arithmetic teachers may explain addition through examples, and ask children to memorize the addition facts. They are then challenged to show skill in using them on numerical problems. Finally, they're called upon to use the process on problems which might occur in everyday life. Although the teacher tries to ensure understanding from the very beginning, the students often spend so much time and effort memorizing the facts that addition becomes rote learning for many of them.

This is the deductive approach to teaching and learning, moving from general principles to applications. But students often find generalizations difficult to understand until they've had lots of contact with specifics. This approach is not as effective as its opposite. But I'm not here to give a disquisition on the inductive/deductive dichotomy.

The issue challenges teachers often, though. It's efficient to present principles first. Rules of French grammar can be stated and demonstrated, followed by practice speaking and writing. Inferring them from much conversation is time-consuming. Physics principles are taught, and then applied in lab work. The original study which led to their development would be hard to replicate. In history, should we learn names, dates, and events first; or the trends and influences they reveal?

I remember an incident when I was a student in France. A young man asked me what the rule was in English for whether to use the simple past tense or the compound past tense. I simply had no idea, but the question nagged at me, and I spent three days trying out usages until I found the answer. Can such an approach be practical at school? And in what subjects?

Much teaching starts with the presentation of information, followed by the acquisition and practice of skills, leading hopefully to some degree of understanding.

The five types of objectives I've just presented will now be used as a framework for further discussion. All education activities should be designed to result in progress toward one or more of them. I'll try to show how to define them in the best way to help teachers plan and teach.

11. Planning and conducting experimental efforts

This section is going to be brief because the topic is so broad, and the approaches one can take are so numerous. Efforts can range from one teacher trying something new to find out what happens to a nation-wide study involving thousands of people and years of work. The approach can be as simple as trial-and-error or as esoteric as investigation into the very nature of learning.

All efforts to innovate, though, reflect the same principle—having an idea, putting it into practice, describing the changes that occur, and making use of any success Studies increase in size and duration mainly because there's a desire to gain greater dependability or influence education more broadly. For my purpose, which is to consider possible changes in school programs and practices, I'll focus on two challenges—how to decide what to focus on and how to do something about it. The first usually involves canvassing current thought and activities, and the latter, making a planned effort to innovate.

In doing the first, all kinds of information can be sought—what works well, what others are thinking and doing, what a review of the professional literature reveals. Procedures can involve questionnaires, interviews, observation, sitting in a library or before a computer screen. These are all straightforward, commonsense ways of searching, and they can all successfully obtain the information needed to produce a worthwhile idea. I've already remarked that good ideas are where you find them. Very commonly, they arise from an individual's personal experience or from witnessing the success of others.

I'll not detail the various methods of canvassing for ideas. They're fairly straightforward, are described in countless textbooks, and demonstrated in many doctoral dissertations. Sometimes, though, an effort to increase one's confidence in the information obtained can lead to extremely painstaking work and the process can become onerous.

Areas of focus for a study can vary widely. A single teacher might look for new classroom procedures, new materials or equipment, new outcomes to focus upon, new methods of evaluation, or what have you? Groups of teachers might be concerned with changes in the syllabus or curriculum, new approaches to evaluating instruction, or ways of getting parents more successfully involved. Eventually an educator, or a group of them, settles on something that appears promising, and decides to try it out. This is the focus of my next remarks.

If it's an instructional change, one teacher may simply decide to do it alone. Often, though, it will be a joint project of a faculty, or a portion of it, usually with the support of the school's administration. Indeed, no one should try innovate, especially if the approach is in any way controversial, without this support.

Frequently, a study just takes the form of simply doing something new to see what happens, with as much care as possible. This requires two elements—a way to describe or measure any improvement and a way to compare it to prior achievement. The most respected method of doing this is the matched-group study, comparing results obtained in two groups—one, experimental, and one, control.

This is seldom practical in a school setting, though, and the usual effort one sees is a single-group experiment, involving one class only. In this case, the "control" group is virtual, and does not exist in reality. Instead, it's created from the teacher's past records or personal recollections. Or perhaps the accomplishment of the class being studied is compared with that of other "normal" ones.

In either case, the control group is created almost out of thin air. The matching is approximate at best, and may not even have been studied at all. If so, any improvement by the experimental group might be the result of other factors than the practice under study. For this reason, the findings of a single-group experiment are frequently dismissed as little better than anecdotal data.

Still, the approach is the foundation of much educational change. It's easy to do in a single class, and if the teacher has kept careful records in the past, and if there's no reason to believe the experimental group differs greatly from earlier classes or those of other teachers, the chance of a result being reliable is very good. Multiply efforts of this kind by the thousands, and you have an engine of change.

The single-group experiment is what I shall concentrate on. I'll assume that any effort to innovate involves no more than a single school, and often no more than a single class, and suggest ways of proceeding that will improve the reliability of outcomes.

The first thing to do is keep good records before starting any innovation. If you're trying to improve subject-matter achievement, you need before-and-after testing of one or more prior classes, as well as of the experimental one, using the same or equivalent tests, so that the amount of progress made in each can be compared. You should also have a record of the age, gender, and I.Q. (or GPA) of each student in every class involved. Comparing the range of these in the different groups can reveal any marked variance which might affect results. The more differences that exist, the less confidence you'll have in your findings.

If you're studying an outcome that's not subject-matter oriented, a similar process should occur. You'll still need age, gender, and I.Q. (or GPA) data, so you can judge if any of these attributes might explain any result. But you'll also need appropriate information about the area of your emphasis, in a manner analogous to the subject-matter testing I just mentioned. This adds the problem that measurement in non-subject-matter fields is not as well developed as customary standardized tests, and you may have to use existing instruments of doubtful validity, or create your own. As a result, you may end up with findings that fail to demonstrate clear-cut improvement.

Clearly, the message I send is to be careful. But since any effort to acquire new knowledge is a leap in the dark, getting some light can only help. And if specialized assistance is available to you, use it. Doing something is often better than sticking with the status quo.

I assume you'll select promising ideas only after much reflection, make your plans the same way, and conduct your study likewise. If you're part of a group study, keep your lines of communication open at all times, and never go off on your own. Indeed, even in a single-class study, it's wise to share your ideas and findings with others, to benefit from their thoughts. Special care must always be taken in assessing results, since the effectiveness of your study is totally dependent on your evaluation procedures. If they are weak, your findings will impress no one. The following sections focus on the evaluation process.

At this point, I should admit that the above is an inadequate description of how an experimental study should proceed. But since I'm not writing a book on research methodology, it will have to do. I'm trying to provide a simple sketch of how one needs to proceed, and I assume that anyone undertaking an experiment will acquire and practice as much good procedure as she or she is comfortable with—recognizing that greater pains increase the likelihood of dependable results. In the Appendix, I wander through the vagaries of a study designed to approximate what a typical group of teachers might actually do.

I'll now reiterate my principal points.

1. Keep the best possible records of the outcome you're seeking to foster.

2. Keep records of factors, like age, gender, and GPA, that might influence results.

3. Acquire any needed skill to the greatest level of that you're comfortable with.

4. Do everything possible to ensure your evaluation procedures meet professional standards.

5. Involve other people.

12. Criteria for evaluation

Now it's time to get down to the nitty-gritty, by showing how to create statements which are actually helpful for classroom practice and effective evaluation.

For example, it's one thing to say we want students to have good moral values. It's another to say we want them to be honest. It's still more explicit to say they shouldn't cheat. What's most useful, though, are statements like "Doesn't copy from other students during an examination," 'Admits his own mistakes," "Doesn't tell dirty jokes," or "Doesn't comment on anyone's sexual activities."

"Knows what 7x9 equals" is much better than "Can do multiplication." We must be quite explicit if we wish everyone to look for the same thing. Of course, the end-result is that the number of statements is vastly increased as we make them more specific.

Let me refer to Dr. Tyler once more. He addressed the issue of defining an objective effectively. It should be worded, he said, not only in a way which precisely specifies the behavior of one who has achieved it, but also, for it to be sufficiently specific, should identify the circumstances in which the behavior is to be demonstrated.

So teachers who wish the learning gained in their classes to carry over into later life need to teach that way, seeking to ensure that transfer actually occurs. To be useful for this, "Doesn't copy on examinations" might become "Doesn't present another person's work as one's own." All life-oriented objectives should be described specifically for specific situations. Instead of "Is a good citizen," use "Votes in elections" or "Reads about political issues." Only in this way can one hope for transfer. And achievements in such areas should not simply be made part of a student's grade. They should be recorded and reported separately.

Most statements of objectives that we see today need to be more precise to apply in practice. This is easy enough when referring to information and skills. "Knows the main issues of the Civil War" or "Can give a summary of Dickens' novels" state exactly what to expect. Likewise, skills such as "Can add a column of whole numbers" or "Is able to translate English into correct French" tell us what to look for.

Since we require students to demonstrate knowledge and skills upon demand, objectives like these are the mainstay of subject-matter goals. And since they're expressed clearly, we can create tests and choose assignments easily. This is why it's done so much. Other objectives are a different matter. Understandings, habits, and values present challenges with increasing levels of difficulty.

Understandings join information and skills as a mainstay of subject fields, although it's sometimes difficult to distinguish between possessing a skill and understanding it. Witness the girl trying to price a tank of gas. Unfortunately, it's too easy to acquire some skills in a rote manner, without really knowing why and how they work.

Still, we think we know what it means to understand something. But consider the statement, "Understands the importance of the Civil War." Does this mean an ability to show the relative importance of battles and campaigns? Does it mean knowing the forces and factors which led to the war's outbreak, and how they influenced it? A student could answer a question about the importance of the Civil War either way, and with material ranging from rote memory to rich understanding. The first interpretation is certainly more mechanistic than the second. One shows possession of a set of facts, the other reveals greater understanding.

Habits are something more. Developing criteria dealing with them presents one of the most challenging tasks a person can undertake. Evidence of habit patterns is elusive and subject to differences of interpretation. Frequently, there's little agreement about when an observed behavior is habitual.

We know that behaviors seen repeatedly can be recognized as a person's characteristic. Every teacher finds that study habits become predictable. Some students procrastinate, some take a long time getting organized, some fiddle around or are easily distracted, some distract others. A teacher becomes aware of the continuing habits of at least some students.

I spent considerable space earlier discussing the habits we wish to encourage, so I'll not repeat that here. What I shall say is that everyone involved with educating children needs to think long and hard about this matter. We need to decide when a pattern of behavior becomes a habit, and when it doesn't.

To use good study habits again as an example. First, there should be consensus about the specific behaviors involved. Until this occurs, no two teachers will have exactly the same priorities, no two will stress the same things, or make the same observations. But once a consensus is reached, observing and recording behavior on a comparable basis can take place. This will be discussed in the next section.

Finally, we come to the question of values. Everything I've said about formulating objectives certainly applies here too. There must be agreement, not only on which values should be stressed, but how their possession can be objectively determined.

Let's use "Has good moral values" as an example again. Any effort to decide the behaviors which reveal these can easily morph into other goal-areas. For instance, "Doesn't cheat" overlaps conscientiousness and honesty. And of course, statements can get more and more specific. "Doesn't say or do anything immoral" is useful. "Doesn't pass false rumors" can be more easily applied.

I hope I've sufficiently illustrated the degree of specificity needed. As you can see, it's not easy to do, and it's certainly subjective. Yet, it's essential if we're to determine students' attainments. Everyone must know what constitutes an acceptable statement, must be in agreement on what to observe, and agree that the information thus obtained is a valid indicator of the objective's acquisition.

13. Evaluation procedures

There are basically three ways to get needed information—asking questions, observing behavior, and judging products or performance. I'll consider each of these, although some attention has already been paid to the first in Chapter Six, where I discuss teachers' test usage. In addition, there's more in the Appendix, where I go through the process of planning and conducting an experimental program.

The basic task is to develop procedures and instruments for assessing and recording student achievement. It's simple common sense to know that once a school determines its objectives, it must find out how much progress it makes toward reaching them.

Asking questions. This is by far the commonest way to find out what students have learned. Easy and familiar, it includes homework assignments, classroom querying, and the quizzes, tests, and exams we all know. It's particularly appropriate for determining the acquisition of information, skills, and understandings. Put simply, we try to find out what students have learned by simply asking them.

This approach, though, doesn't ensure that what's obtained is what's most important. Sometimes, it's only what's easiest, and if so, the school's goals may be at least partially determined by the instruments used, and reflect simpler rather than more complex outcomes.

The objective examination is widely criticized as revealing only a lower form of learning. It shows students' ability to recognize information, but not to recall it upon demand. This distinction between recognition and recall is best illustrated by a person's vocabulary. We all know many words when we see or hear them that we never use in our own writing and speech. The first is recognition, the second, recall.

But in a subject-field where knowledge of many facts and skills are expected, teachers often use an objective test because it can cover ground efficiently, even though its results may reflect fortunate guesses. Measuring more advanced skills and understandings requires other forms of testing. Ways to do this have already been discussed

Objective-test writers have sometimes tried to address more advanced learnings by creating items that ask students to weigh pieces of information presented to them, and choose justified conclusions from among several listed alternatives. This approach can be used in subjects like literature and history, where no right-and-wrong answers may exist and deep understanding is valued. Presumably, what's revealed is more than simple recognition of correct information.

Finally, for those who believe the essay test—so widely admired and so easy to misuse—is the answer, let me reflect on it once more. In a famous incident many years ago, an individual charged with rating students' performance on the New York State Regents examination created an outline of what he considered to be the perfect answer to an essay question. Through mischance, this sheet fell into the hands of another evaluator, who, assuming it to be a candidate's effort, read it and gave it a failing grade. At that point, according to policy, it was rated additionally by several others. Their grades ranged from failing to 100 percent.

The story shows how necessary it is to obtain consensus, especially about the role of English skills in other subjects. This too was dealt with in Chapter Six, so I'll limit myself to saying that essay tests should be used only when there's agreement on how to grade them.

To sum up, it's not easy to do testing, especially if one wants to distinguish among levels of learning. And since most teachers are not skilled in test construction, special efforts must be made to offset this limitation. If the procedure can't be relied upon, it is seriously flawed.

Judging products and performances. Essays are products, so of course I've just been discussing this aspect of evaluation. However, I use the word, product, to refer to something created by a student, possibly of his of her own volition, like creating a picture, writing a story, making a bookcase, preparing a meal, or building a machine. The end-result must be examined and evaluated by someone knowledgeable, usually the teacher.

Performances, too, need to be assessed by competent raters, through observation and/or listening. Debating, playing an instrument, cheer-leading, acting in a play—all call for judgments like those for essays or other products. Athletic performance is in a class by itself.

This kind of assessment is extremely subjective and extremely difficult. But we shouldn't be too surprised, though, if we've watched judges at the Olympics rate divers, ice-skaters, and gymnasts. Sizable groups of experts, many of them former outstanding performers, vary widely in their scores, even though using carefully-drawn descriptions of behavior.

Aren't we asking teachers to do something similar—only, of course, with criteria which are not drawn nearly so well? Indeed, they're often not drawn at all, or drawn individually by each evaluator. Almost everything I said about grading essays is appropriate here. We must reach agreement on what we're looking for. We need consensus, with clear criteria, so everyone can get similar results.

Some say athletics are different, in that contests are performances decided by winners and losers, and that this is certainly evaluation. Of course, this is true. But goals in physical education are about more than winning and losing. Otherwise, we'd grade students by timing them, or matching them in competition. Coaches know that evaluating athletes is more than picking winners. Those who draft for the N.F.L. certainly do. As do parents of P.E. students.

Using school objectives to create criteria for judging products and performances is a staggering task. Confusion and misinterpretation, subjectivity, use of inappropriate or incorrect elements, or failure to use correct ones, all can lead to mistakes. But we can do no less. We must try.

Observation of behavior. As we move into non-academic outcomes like values and habits, the need for observation becomes obvious. How else can students show these except by what they do and say? And who are to be the knowledgeable observers? Usually, the teachers.

There's much uncertainty and disagreement about the values and habits of a fully-functioning adult. I'll assume the school has a vested interest in the social and moral performance of students, and this mandates that educators take positive action to observe, and report to parents. Yet even when a school wants to help students develop desirable values and habits, we really don't know if it does. And we should.

Student behavior is seldom recorded or reported today, except in very general terms, and mainly when the behavior has been unconstructive. Often this is the principal contact between the home and the school on non-academic matters. We must do more. If non-academic objectives are a part of education, there's an obligation for the school to plan jointly with the home.

Observation of behavior is rarely done in any systematic or objective way, probably because of its difficulty. But the challenge is as important as it is difficult. It simply can't be done by testing or questioning. Although students could conceivably be asked to express their beliefs about honesty, cooperation, etc., there's little reason to believe their responses would be valid, perhaps because the respondent hasn't done that much self-examination, or feels this is a private matter, or wants to pretend. As for tests, there aren't any, at least for most virtues treasured by society.

What else do we use, then, other than observation—watching behavior in the classroom and elsewhere? Teachers see students every day, and get accustomed to their habits. Indeed, they often see little else. They are the ones to rely upon to do the job. While more reliable results might be obtained by trained observers in a controlled lab situation, this approach is clearly not practical in a school.

Observations must be recorded when they occur, and the records placed in a folder. Eventually the school, and the parents, will possess a picture of a student's typical behavior. Over time, it should begin to reveal his or her values and habits. So let's identify desirable behaviors, without decreeing what they represent. Indeed, teachers do this all the time, as they establish rules for classroom behavior.

But the process is not only highly subjective, there's great difficulty in agreeing on what to look for, and how to quantify the findings. There's a double challenge—reaching consensus and helping teachers become good observers.

Getting consensus often becomes involved with disputes over semantics—people interpreting terms differently. This difficulty can be sidestepped by starting with behaviors rather than generalities. Even if there's disagreement about the nature of conscientiousness or honesty or whatever, and the behaviors which reveal them, people can probably agree on a number of actions they consider to be constructive. Simply keeping an accurate record of these, without trying to define what they add up to, should yield useful information. If later, someone cares to name the attribute that's been revealed, so be it. But in any event, it reveals a pattern of desirable behavior.

To illustrate, if we're concerned about social sensitivity, we can create a tentative list (to be changed through experience), of actions which might reflect this or its converse. But as we proceed, and as we amend the list, our information should reach a point where we can predict with confidence how a student will act toward other people, and can say how socially sensitive he or she is.

As for becoming good observers, the answer is improving the descriptions of behavior to be looked for, sharing observational experiences and learnings, relying on expert help, and practice, practice, practice.

In summary, I've presented various ways of getting information about student attainment, some in current use, some not. Many of those in use are not being done very well. Later, I'll suggest a program of evaluation. My basic position is that schools must constantly seek evidence about progress toward all important outcomes, using the best means possible.

PART FIVE

Changing the System

14. What do we need to change?

In Part Two, I suggested what to do within the school as it's presently constituted. There's a limit, though, to how much improvement can take place this way. I feel the need to go further, and say what major changes are needed if we are to have the educational system which we, and our children, deserve.

There are six areas where I believe serious thought should be given to change: 1) the five practices I discussed in Part Two, 2) the curriculum, 3) the evaluation and reporting of student achievement, 4) the organization of the educational structure, and 5) the education profession itself.

15. Five flawed practices

I'll start by returning briefly to the five practices I deplore: 1) teaching as "telling," 2) improper use of homework. 3) inadequate treatment of reading deficiencies, 4) the ABCDF system of grading, and 5) poor testing practices. If I didn't think these needed major change, I wouldn't have written this book. But what more can I say that I haven't said already?

Only that there's a big difference between change in a single classroom or school and that which occurs more broadly. My earlier comments were directed at the first of these two. I now wish to look at the second.

Any of the suggestions I made then could be the focus of research or an experimental study, and attract serious attention. If instituted widely it could become an element of major change. It's up to the broken-front approach to determine how widespread this influence might be.

Each of the five has one or more groups of individuals especially concerned with it. And everyone might have issues. Instructional methods, homework usage, and testing practices are such a part of teachers' very being as to be widely resistant to change It might well take some time, as well as being stressed in teacher-education programs. It's widely believed that important developments in education take about fifty years to gain widespread acceptance. That's about the amount of time needed to replace one generation of teachers with another.

But the administration, the community, and the parents all have their areas of concern. Parents are especially impacted by homework policies, and any changes would require their widespread support, and might involve the community as well. As for the administration, it's involved in everything

Of course, any major change requires widespread support, but especially if it has to do with the grading system. This area simply demands it. Everyone will want to get into the act. On the other hand, a decision to create special programs for dealing with reading deficiencies can be made administratively. And almost certainly, it would be warmly welcomed by parents. As for state mandates or federal projects involving the use of standardized tests, no school or district can do much more than simply accept them.

Now I'd like to address other areas that in my opinion require major change.

16. The curriculum

I'll start with the curriculum. This is the very heart of education. It truly is the way by which we designate what we want our children to learn. And we must be convinced that it provides the best possible results. This challenge presents two questions: 1) Are we teaching everything we should? 2) Are we teaching anything we shouldn't?

I've already remarked that some aspects of the curriculum have not been reexamined for many years. We assume we already know what's important for children to learn. But do we really?

Many years ago (1939), Dr. Harold Benjamin (under the pen name, J. Abner Peddiwell) wrote an enchanting little volume called *The Saber-Tooth Curriculum,* which is no less appropriate today than it was then. It tells the story of cave dwellers, living as hunters and gatherers, who wanted an educational program for their children. They chose to include such useful matters as catching fish with bare hands, clubbing tiny horses, and frightening saber-tooth tigers with torches.

Centuries later, conditions had changed. Fish were caught with nets, tiny horses had died out, and the tigers were no more. But their schools still taught the same old "solid" subjects. They had "cultural" values, and were justified by saying that fish-catching developed muscular coordination, horse-clubbing engendered stealth and ingenuity, and tiger-scaring built courage. Anyone who wanted to teach something new and practical, like net-making, snaring, or trapping was considered radical.

Benjamin's point is obvious. No matter how valuable a learning area was originally, it needs to reestablish its worth from time to time. If its original purpose has disappeared, data must be collected to show that it successfully achieves any new outcome advanced to justify its continued existence. But we don't do this. Instead, we behave just like our ancient ancestors.

Society has changed over the years, and there are many new needs. But these are not given the same emphasis as older ones. New proposals, even those dedicated to a capability clearly valuable to society, like child-rearing or money management, must justify their existence. This is not required of established courses.

I suggest that we rethink why we teach any subject. And we should look not only at its value for further education, but its worth in later life as well. Let's consider anew what we want our schools to do.

When students graduate from high school, what should they be prepared for? Of course, we want many of them to be ready for college. What about the others? Should they also receive preparation for an institution they won't attend? Perhaps this learning is equally useful in the outside world? But is it?

Should young people receive specific help to become good workers, good citizens, and good family members? Do those going on to higher education also need this training? If they do, do we believe they'll get it later? We know better. Whatever help of this kind is received by college students, it's very hit or miss. I've previously reported that one of the most important learnings of my entire life occurred in the very last course I took in my doctoral program. That's much too late.

I once heard the dean of a state university's College of Arts and Sciences answer the question, "How is a student who gets a degree in your college better prepared to enter society?" His response, "That's an improper thing to ask. The arts and sciences are their own reason for existing."

So, when we determine what young people need to know to enter society, we need to think about college-bound students as well as the others. This requires us to include areas of learning which lie beyond the standard academic subjects. You may say that we've already done much of this, that many parts of our present curriculum represent new areas of learning. But these do not have the same prestige or staying power as college-prep subjects, nor do they furnish graduation requirements to anything like the same extent.

Planning a system of universal education—one in which all students are educated to an optimum level of their talents, and appropriate to their needs—faces at least three goals: 1) students' preparation to continue their education, 2) their readiness to enter the workplace, and 3) their possession of the values, habits, and abilities needed for life in society. At present, these three are intermingled, and no one can say our schools have optimum success in all of them. Some might even say, not any of them.

The "solid" subjects. These dominate the high-school curriculum and graduation requirements. We were all taught within this framework, with the result that the public generally is convinced that a grounding in the solid subjects is the foundation of a good education. This is held to be true for everyone, including students not going beyond high school, and even for those who drop out. The primacy of the solid subjects is rarely questioned. They have been sanctified by tradition.

I've already pointed out how parents with high expectations for their children want the high school to provide as much college-prep work as possible. And for years, colleges did have specific subject-matter requirements for admission, making an enormous impact on secondary education.

But college expectations have changed in recent years, with ever-increasing emphasis on factors beyond school performance. More and more often, statements of entrance requirements suggest that applicants pursue a balanced high-school program with academic subjects well represented. I see no sign, though, that this diminishes any parents' desire for more solid subjects in the high school, and especially, advanced-placement courses. They want all this, with anything additional expected by colleges simply added to their list of concerns.

One consequence of all this has been that many students not going to college take subjects they might not have chosen otherwise. There's often comfort with this because of the belief that even if the content isn't useful in later life, there'll be transfer of training from subject achievement to real-world challenges. But considerable evidence exists that such transfer occurs only when there's true similarity between the field of learning and the field of application. If this were not the case, philosophy majors could be expected to take leading roles in business and politics.

Another consequence is that required academic courses, often simply the early stages of college subjects, occupy so much curricular space that other areas can't squeeze in. Anyone considering a new course must be prepared to show that its worth is at least as great as that of geometry or physics, or some other required subject.

The solid subjects are certainly here to stay. But I ask if long-standing college entrance requirements haven't become the tail that wags the dog. I say this, not to disparage any person or institution, but to highlight my belief that society has come to accept reverse logic. We've come to accept the role of the public schools as primarily one of preparation for advanced work, rather than seeing higher education as part of an overall plan.

If we're to look afresh at American education, we must take into account the needs of students for whom high school is a final stage, as well as the others. Parents of college-bound students are influential, but their concerns should not be overpowering. Other parents have expectations too. Possibly, their main desire is for the schools to prepare their children for the world of work. Does a highly academic program do this best? We need to rethink the value of solid subjects for these young people.

This does not require comparing subjects so much as it calls for looking at course outcomes, and choosing those which are most appropriate. Possibly, all that's needed is turning a required course into an elective. Although It would arouse a firestorm of controversy if any school in America should try to eliminate a core subject, or major part of it, or remove it from graduation requirements.

Are we correct in believing academic programs and graduation requirements meet the needs of the non-college-bound student as well as they should? Let's not assume we already know. Instead, let's get evidence.

I'll start with English, because I feel it's the most defensible. There's widespread agreement that young people should be able to use our language well. At the same time, we hear many complaints about poor grammar of graduates, and their sloppy habits of writing and speaking. Do we apportion students' time appropriately? Is there too much emphasis on literature and not enough on proper usage? And why don't we spend more time on the skills of speaking in public?

Answering these questions goes beyond the scope of this book. But I advance them as examples of what needs to be looked at. The role of English in the life of an effective adult should be examined to determine what its main emphases in the curriculum should be. We should also consider the needs of those for whom it is a second language.

Mathematics is a different matter entirely. Even as we see colleges complain that many incoming students require remediation, we also see less and less use of computational skills in the real world. We've become so used to having transactions handled by machines that cashiers are helpless if their computers crash. Calculators and computers have changed our lives. What does that mean for mathematics in the curriculum?

My late wife once told a story about a workshop she conducted for junior-high-school teachers. During the open-question time she was asked, "Dr. Bebell, how can we get seventh-graders interested in algebra?" She asked in return, "Why do you want to do that?" And was told, "Many of our students drop out of school by ninth grade, and if they aren't given algebra early, they'll never get it."

There you are. To planners in that school there was no question that algebra was worthwhile, even for dropouts. They were concerned only about how to get it done. But, for such students, I see no point in it whatsoever. And I can't be charged with anti-math bias. I majored in it in college, and taught it for a number of years. But how can algebra be u

Furthermore, shouldn't we look at how early in a child's life arithmetic is introduced. Do we really believe it should be taught in the first grade, or even kindergarten, when it was once a college course? And if we do, why do we? I know we start very gently, yet math proficiency is gained slowly and painstakingly at an early age, while later on it can be mastered very quickly. The National Council of Teachers of Mathematics has done a great deal to make the early study of arithmetic as child-friendly as possible. Is more needed? Is its early introduction the best use of student time?

Mathematics is truly in need of rethinking. What part of it does today's adult need in everyday life or the world of work? Perhaps its appropriateness is limited to preparation for college or for certain jobs or specializations. Is its preeminence in the curriculum due to tradition?

As for science and the social studies, much of what I've just said is relevant for them. Clearly, people need to be familiar with the elements of history, geography, and civics, if they are to be effective citizens. Also, many aspects of physics, chemistry, biology, and geology are of value. But which learnings are needed, and for what purpose? Like math and English, these areas should be revisited.

I've said that the life-needs of students should take precedence over the needs of colleges. And this might not be such a bad thing for those institutions themselves. Is it possible that a student who acquires a love of learning and the skills of critical thinking will do well anywhere in higher education? Might it be that transcript specifics are immaterial?

Many years ago, a group of schools conducted a project called the Eight-Year Study. It's now almost erased from memory, even of those who were alive in the 30's, and is probably unknown to most educators active today. It was an amazing experiment. Some thirty secondary schools around the country took charge of their own programs, and many prestigious colleges and universities agreed to accept their graduates without regard to conventional entrance requirements. This was done for four years, and the participants tracked for another four years. A follow-up study was also made twenty years later.

One basic finding, quoted from its report in 1942, was that "...success in the college of liberal arts does not depend upon the study of certain subjects for a certain period in high school." Students from the experimental schools did at least as well as a matched group of students who met entrance requirements conventionally. Of course, the analysis went into many kinds of outcomes, and results varied a little among them. But the clear finding was that adherence to college requirements did not produce a better group of students than allowing high schools to do their own thing.

Unfortunately, the project's report appeared as World War II was breaking out, and America had other things on its mind than education. Consequently, the results did not attract a lot of attention, and after the war were already old news. Perhaps it's time for another study, to compare the success of students from schools planning new programs with those from traditional schools.

I'd like to see a debate of the relative value of geography and parenting skills for someone destined to factory or service work. For that matter, why not a debate on the relative value of Shakespeare or more study of grammar and syntax for the college-bound student?

I know the solid subjects have a hammerlock on the school's program. But should they be mandatory? Or what part of them should be mandatory ? is it conceivable that college-prep courses might become elective?

I've made my point. The solid subjects need re-justification, not only in terms of their contribution to students' readiness for continued education, but also for vocational success and life in society.

Newer areas of study. Much of the foregoing discussion implies that areas of study other than the solid subjects need to be considered for the curriculum. And I've shown that I believe these areas are related to the problems of daily life.

There are so many things the effective adult needs to do well. Any list of the competences which are needed is so extensive as to overwhelm my powers to enumerate. The home, family, workplace, neighborhood, community, and citizenship all call for skills.

There is much we have to do well, like:
child-rearing
money management
householding
cooking
driving and automobile maintenance.

We're called on to be:
  good workers
  good family members
  good friends
  good participants in activities

We're expected to get along well with others, and generally be a credit to society. And all this says nothing about moral and spiritual practices, good health habits, charitable endeavors, and much else, including self-awareness and understanding of others.

Once again, who is to say geography is a more important learning than parenting skills? I know how valuable geography can be, but how important is child-rearing? I chose this comparison earlier, since for many persons the answer is self-evident. Similar comparisons might include chemistry vs. auto mechanics, or plane geometry vs. money management. In each case, we assume the first is more valuable than the second. But is it? Such questions should be taken seriously.

In recent years, many non-academic subjects have appeared in schools, including home economics (however it's named), industrial arts, driver education, sex education (also under many names), citizenship, psychology, and others. There are also the quasi-standard subjects like physical education, art, music, foreign languages, business education. I call them "quasi," because they're more likely to be eliminated or cut back than English, math, science, and social studies, when budget crunches occur.

The non-academic subjects listed above at least have gained a toehold. But think of all the others. Take parenting skills for example. Many of these have to be learned the hard way. We see out-of-control, inexperienced parents abusing children, because they don't know better, or can't exercise self-control, or both. How can society justify not helping prepare new parents? We require training and a license for a person to cut hair, but everyone is presumed able to rear a child.

Earlier, I presented a partial list of the capabilities essential for life in society. Although there's been some experimentation with some of these in some places, we don't see them play a large role in formal education. But surely such important abilities can be acquired more quickly, easily, and effectively with educational help.

The preceding seems to suggest a need to compare academic learnings with non-academic. But I don't believe this is an either-or circumstance. We need both kinds, and it is the college-bound student who has the more difficult choices to make, since it is that individual for whom the solid subjects may preclude other learnings.

As for those not going to college, we should plan specifically for them, instead of just fitting them into existing programs. And their graduation requirements should be adjusted accordingly. Vocational education courses are often offered for such students, but these are frequently not as useful as they hope since they tend to lag behind technical advance.

I've presented four main areas to look for new courses: 1) family and home, 2) community and social life, 3) the world of work, and 4) desirable personal qualities. Many people would disagree about which, if any, of them to consider. I'll not make additional specific recommendations than I've already given.

Terminal secondary education. If we do what I suggest, we say in effect that the schools' primary responsibility is to society, and not to higher education. The end-result of this would be to turn the high-school experience into terminal education. Every graduate would be expected to possess a preparedness for life, including those going on to higher education. College-prep work would be an elective extra.

Isn't this really the main duty of public education—turning out humans well equipped to enter society? Shouldn't this attainment be equally valuable for those who continue their education? The colleges would certainly benefit from a student body composed of capable adults.

What can take priority over this? How can we allow children to grow up and enter adult life without getting all the help they need? Why do we believe that what we now require is more useful to them than what is needed in the real world? At the very least, let's have representative groups of citizens rank present high-school offerings and proposed life-skills programs in value to society. We might be surprised.

Terminal secondary education implies that some high-school graduates might not possess the normal prerequisites for higher education. But if they possess such attributes as love of learning, problem-solving ability, and reliance upon evidence to make decisions, they should be capable college students. The Eight-Year Study showed us that.

In brief, the schools of the future must place education for life at least on a par with preparation for college, and restructure their curriculum accordingly.

Possible studies and activities. Here are some suggestions which might stimulate thought and change.

Canvass older adults, asking what influence the solid subjects in high school had on their lives.

Ask students to report anonymously their opinion of the value of various courses, and why they believe as they do.

Examine the content of high-school courses to determine what's useful for non-college-bound students.

Review college admission requirements to see what subject-matter mandates they have, and how much variation exists.

Develop a set of goals representing the qualities we desire in a young adult in our society.

Survey members of the community, to discover how much value they believe various new course offerings might have.

Create a new course, for example, Household Responsibilities, to see how much interest it attracts and how much success it has.

Survey the professional literature to find new areas to consider for the curriculum.

17. The program of evaluation

I've already noted the deficiencies of the ABCDF grading system, and what might be done to improve it. I now want to speak about replacing the whole system.

Not only is it fundamentally defective, it's a major cause of what's wrong in education. It steers students away from learning anything not on a test. It invites last-minute cramming, known for emphasizing ephemeral learnings that quickly vanish. It interferes with cooperative group work. And it destroys the motivation of slower learners

Our job in education is to help all students reach their best level of achievement. This is hard to do if we tell them over and over how inferior they are. I've already beat this drum, so I'll say no more.

I know parent-teacher conferences are supposed to pick up the slack, but generally any information provided then is verbal, with no written record, and is often forgotten or misremembered. I also know some schools now provide some descriptive material about a student's behavior and habits, but this varies from place to place, is often sketchy, and frequently uses terms which are ill-defined or not defined at all.

Since a letter grade is an inadequate and incomplete description, with widespread disagreement on what any grade means, I see little reason for the continued use of this system other than to spur students to work harder. But I've tried to show this usage turns learning into a rat race, and for many into a disaster.

What should be looked at? Clearly, we have to report accurately what every student has learned. Without doubt, this will reveal high achievement of some students and poor work of others. But it can be done without invidious comparisons, and without labeling anyone as a failure. I'm convinced almost everyone learns at least something.

Let's report the precise amount each student has learned and leave it at that. We can identify the essential learnings of a subject-field, and say how much of this has been acquired. Whether this is reported as a percent of the total body of learning, or is a score on a competency scale, or in some other way, is immaterial. But let the results speak for themselves. If students or parents wish to compare these, it's up to them. But everyone should something to build on.

I'd like to refer once more to Wrinkle's book, *Improving Marking and Reporting Practices in Elementary and Secondary Schools.* This little volume, barely 100 pages long, detailed the struggles of a faculty, over a period of ten years, to improve their grading system. I know the book appeared sixty-five years ago, but I've never seen anything better.

Wrinkle reports how his teachers tried to decide what was important enough to report, what was a practical way to get the information, and how to insure the result was reliable and comprehensive. It's a good approach to follow—even today. Perhaps, especially today.

Their approach, and mine, is to recommend that the school provide enough accurate information that anyone reading the material will have a good idea of each student's accomplishments and work habits. Letter-grades don't do this. And information sent with transcripts usually stresses strengths without reference to needs. Often, the language is oddly reminiscent of that found in the remarks of publicists.

But what should be included? Of course, subject-matter achievement should be a main part. It should show what a student knows, understands, and can do in the subject-field. It should not be distorted by any other consideration. But it might well indicate the student's further needs

What else? The record might also contain any information relevant to the student's ability to perform, whether it be at college, in the world of work, or as a citizen, family member, and participant in society. That's a tall order, and requires much trial-and-error. Any school seeking to improve its evaluation program, though, needs to decide what's important enough to be included. Its public statement of educational purposes and objectives should drive the process.

Getting the information. It's one thing to say you need certain information. It's another to get it. This becomes apparent if you notice what is present and not present in the records we keep now.

Many years ago, when I was a teacher in the lab school at Ohio State University, I faced a real challenge. The school did not believe in letter-grades. Instead, they required every teacher to send a letter home three times a year, informing parents of their child's progress. I had no idea how to do this efficiently, or even effectively, but scrabbled together a letter detailing the class' activities generally, the student's activities and accomplishments specifically, and projecting his or her future needs.

When I did this the first time, I was shocked to discover that I didn't have much to say about some of the class members. I had a record of their attendance, their homework, and their test results, but not much else. I hadn't noticed anything unusual, good or bad, about their work habits, their attentiveness, or their interaction with other students. They'd just not done anything in class which attracted my attention sufficiently for me to remember it later. Although I'd seen each one every day, some had not really become three-dimensional human beings in my mind. The ablest students I had definitely noticed, and those experiencing difficulties had stood out clearly, but almost half the class had gotten lost in what I came to call the great, gray middle.

Needless to say, this taught me a lesson. From then on, I kept a folder on every student, and after each class session would drop a short note in two or three, detailing something I'd observed. Then, about halfway through the term, I checked to see which folders didn't have many observations. I'd concentrate on these in the remaining time. I note that the making of such anecdotal notes is now encouraged.

I tell this story to show how difficult data-gathering can be. Yet it's essential that information be as complete, objective, and unambiguous as possible, so any user of the resulting report will have a meaningful description of the student, and how he or she might be expected to perform.

Testing will probably always be used to determine subject-matter achievement, but it should be done differently from how it's done today. I've already spent considerable space on test construction, and tried to show that when teachers are responsible for their own tests, confusion and variability are inevitable. We have hidden from this fact, assuming everyone's assessment is equally valid and reliable, and comparable to everyone else's in the same subject-field. This is just not so.

Comparable instruments should be used by everyone teaching the same course, with agreement on their focus and content. They should be developed to exacting standards of validity and reliability. Items should be reviewed by test specialists, be subjected to analysis, and be stored and protected for further use, so they wouldn't have to be redone every reporting period.

It would take considerable time and effort to create a reservoir of acceptable items with known levels of difficulty. But once done, appropriate tests can be created whenever needed, and identical or comparable ones created for use in sections of the same course. whether contemporaneous or taught at different times.

Any outside examination used as a substitute should be reviewed by the faculty, to ensure it has the same elements and emphases as they had in their classrooms.

Other forms of student achievement necessitate other measures. These too I've also already discussed, including the need for involving learners in the process. Since evaluation must be accepted by them if it is to be truly effective, students should be encouraged to practice self-assessment and helped to do so.

But any school accepting values or habits are part of their responsibility needs to devise ways to determine what's been accomplished. It's indeed difficult to write descriptions of behavior in such clear-cut terms that all observers look for the same thing. Similarly with criteria for judging students' products and performances. In addition to being hard to prepare, such forms of assessment are difficult to use, and subject to controversy. But they need to be tried, and certainly demand consensus.

How should results be reported? I'll end this discussion of evaluation by saying that the whole system of reporting needs to be overhauled. Even if a school is not going to change its grading system, it should provide more information than it does now.

Once an area for evaluation has been chosen, and its method of assessment determined, the form of reporting should follow naturally, and of course depends upon its nature. I've already suggested that subject-matter achievement might be reported as the degree of competence, or percent of mastery. Student behavior might be reported in narrative form, as I had to do at one time, or alternatively, as the frequency with which various habits and practices have been displayed. Specific behaviors which have been observed can be checked off on a list delivered to parents.

Products and performances might be treated either as part of subject-matter achievement when appropriate, or separately on a scale of one to ten, similar to Olympic gymnastics. In either case, it should be described fully. Explanatory material should be provided to anyone for whom a new approach is confusing.

Possible studies and activities. I hope the following might stimulate thought or action.

Create a procedure to measure and report a student's acquisition of good study habits.

Experiment with objective observation of students' social sensitivity.

Devise a way to measure and report subject-matter achievement which is not affected by the student's effort, English usage, and classroom behavior.

Use a pretest to measure student achievement at the beginning of a class, followed by a comparable test at the end, to isolate progress made under a specific teacher.

Develop a subject-matter test of professional quality, suitable for use in diagnosing student needs.

Ask parents what additional information they would like to see on reports.

Solicit faculty opinions on the criteria and procedures that should be used to grade essays.

Describe the classroom behavior, effort, test and homework scores, truancy, grammar and spelling skills, and general messiness of students in a history class, and ask a group of parents to assign a grade to each.

Devise a form for the learner to report his or her success in developing good work habits, and asking what should be involved.

18. Organization of education

We've all been students, so we know what to expect when we visit a school—class size, periods of fixed length, rows of identical rooms, and the customary amenities. We're familiar with semester- or year-long courses with a set number of sessions each week. Most of these arrangements haven't changed much in our lifetime. Like the basic curriculum, we see them as almost immutable. I'm saying they should all be subject to reexamination.

Like the summer break. We know it was originally intended to free students for work on the family farm. Yet we generally still take this time off, although few sons and daughters do farm labor today. This inherited practice needs rethinking, since studies show students lose ground during the summer. Some schools have already taken action, and remain in session the year around. But the usage is by no means common, although it may be growing.

We still have rows of classrooms because that's how we started. We still teach students in groups for the same reason. Likewise, we divide the day into periods of fixed length, the year into semesters, and the curriculum into courses mostly for administrative efficiency. Much of this has existed since time immemorial with little variation. We should re-examine all these, to see if they're still the best way to educate.

A new look is long overdue. We've forgotten that everything must justify its existence—sooner or later. We should restudy everything the way we look at the year-round school. Needless to say, decisions will vary from place to place, based on the curriculum, student needs, and local concerns.

The schedule. Changing the curriculum will change the way we schedule. We should look at every subject to determine how it should be divided into parts. These decisions should be based on the subject's natural structure, not by dividing it arbitrarily like the countries of Africa. Not every subject needs a year, or even a semester, or five sessions a week.

Some of this is already being done. But arranging it is a lot more complicated than our present practice of five-day-a-week courses for everyone. Still, in these days of computers, anything is possible.

Middle- and high-school programs will continue to be organized around subject areas, but might be structured in other ways than by semesters or years. And many new subjects need to be added. Both developments might require a variety of course lengths

We also might need to schedule special projects for individuals and small groups. And what about the possibility of clustering courses? There's no magic formula specifying the proper amount of exposure to a subject.

I hear many administrators say that this is a scheduling nightmare. In effect, they're implying that if something is difficult, it shouldn't be attempted. But, although change is difficult, rearrangement of schedules is by no means the hardest part. Changing people is the real poser.

If major-league baseball can schedule 162 games for 30 different teams, with different times, dates, places, travel arrangements, home-and-away balance, and a full complement of opponents, for every team, school scheduling problems should be manageable. Have administrators ever really tested the computer's capabilities?

The building. If we're going to address the needs of all students, we'll probably use small groups composed of those who need special treatment, like advanced study or remediation. As well as larger ones where learners can work individually under supervision. And there might be need for office-size spaces where students can get one-on-one help or do independent study.

This variation in group size would make demands on physical facilities, and require greater flexibility than we have at present. Schools have always been built to match the practices and programs in existence, and were designed to last for years. Changes of the kind I suggest might entail major remodeling, or acquisition of additional space.

This raises the question of cost, which is clearly a factor in structural alterations. Of course, every proposal has to face the issue of money, and cost-benefit analysis will always be necessary. In Chapter 9, I discussed financial strictures as an impediment to change. I note that if some study groups were larger, it could save money.

The school district. You make think it presumptuous for me to consider needed change in school districts, since these are so well established, and many have functioned successfully for years. Furthermore, considerable consolidation has taken place in the last century.

This consolidation occurred because many districts were so small they had too much difficulty in providing a good education. So they were often merged to gain the benefits of larger size, and greater financial resources. A sort of partial consolidation has also been seen in the form of boards of cooperative services. These enable several districts to share specialized services which none of them could afford alone.

There are four features of school districts which materially affect their educational program. These are: their size, their approach to central control, difficulties of communication and coordination, and how the school board functions.

Size. Size is a two-edged sword. While it's true that larger districts provide a more comprehensive curriculum, attract better teachers, offer more services, and build better buildings, there's also something lost. Smaller districts with smaller schools tend to possess a treasured place in the community and a closeness between home and school that metropolitan and suburban districts can only envy.

So far as I know, there has rarely been any attempt to downsize an existing school or district. But some districts are gigantic, with a million or more students. Is it possible for a district to be too big?

Or for a school to be too big? We all know that extra-curricular activities are more competitive in larger schools. For example, if a high school is twice the size of another, its athletic teams and many other activities involve a smaller percentage of the student body. It's harder to make the football team, or the cheerleading squad, to appear in a school play, be on the chess team, or stand out in any way.

I once gave a commencement address to the graduating class of a rural high school. There were 17 graduates, the town had a population of 500, and there were 700 people in attendance. The superintendent personally introduced each graduating senior to the audience, recounting his or her achievements in school and plans for the future.

The same year, my daughter graduated from a large urban school. The ceremony required a downtown auditorium. There were 1500 students in her class, with 3000-4000 people in attendance. When diplomas were handed out, four lines were formed in four corners, and four school-board members delivered the diplomas, without any graduate's name being read aloud.

So both smallness and largeness have benefits. We should study ways to get the advantages of both. How can we do more to humanize the huge school and district? How can we get more and better resources to those who are too small and/or remote? Perhaps, there's an optimum size for both districts and schools.

Central control. As school systems get larger, their administration takes on many of the attributes of a state or even a country. The central authority looks and acts increasingly like a ministry of education. Earlier, in discussing the broken-front approach to innovation, I noted that a small centralized group can never be expected to think as creatively, and in as many ways, as a broad array of active minds.

Our largest districts have long struggled with this problem. Often, the demographics of their outlying schools resemble those of the neighboring suburbs more than those of their own inner-city. For this reason, district-wide programs and practices which have a one-size-fits-all quality may be uncomfortable, and even inappropriate, in some parts of the district.

We do see the growing use of magnet schools and charter schools, which can attract students from across the district. Also, some cities have granted considerable autonomy to individual schools, allowing them to plan their own programs for their own students within broad guidelines.

This is certainly an area demanding study and experimentation. All school administrators have the same desire—to provide the best education possible for all their students. So they must be willing to look carefully at centralized decisions, to see how they affect individual schools.

Communication and coordination. A major part of the difficulty of large-district planning is that the very size of the organization creates problems in communicating and coordinating. Representative groups are difficult to assemble. Policy dissemination is often hard to achieve. Even the scheduling of meetings takes time and effort.

To say nothing of "office politics." In every sizable organization, the competition for positions and promotions is intense, and many people and groups feel a need to defend their turf. How much this impedes educational advance is certainly worth study,

I'm sure that there's research on how barriers to communication and coordination affect planning in large endeavors, although I have not seen any specifically aimed to schools. We should look at what we're doing now, to determine how our practices can be improved. Again, there's a probability that size is critical.

The school board. My remarks here are based on extensive personal observation over time. And many of the challenges of operating a school system have not changed greatly through the years.

The school board, elected by the community to implement citizens' wishes for their schools, presumably reflects these wishes, and face the challenge of re-election if it doesn't. It's usually composed of valued members of society, who serve without pay, rarely get thanked, and often get criticized. We should appreciate their willingness to serve.

But frequently, people get elected who are without any special experience with education. And sometimes, persons come on board with an ax to grind. Still, almost all board members I've known, I found to try their best. What I have to say is intended only to be helpful.

First, how do they obtain the information they need to make good decisions? Typically, they rely on the school superintendent, or other professional educators, to provide this. This means the board is usually guided by the understandings, and possibly the priorities of those persons. This is as it should be, in my opinion, since they are employed by the board to run the schools and recommend policies. At the same time, it channels the information that the board receives through an individual or a small group, and may reduce its access to other views.

Sometimes an issue arises where the board, or some of its members, takes a position at variance from that of the superintendent. This has the potential to create a problem. What to do?

Probably the best thing is to get help. If the issue is controversial, and especially when strong feelings are involved, the best approach usually is to seek consensus rather than force a decision. This is a time for qualified outside advisors to provide authentic information about the pro's and con's of an issue.

Indeed, supplementary help is often a board's best resource for help in making all major decisions. Even a matter which is not controversial may be difficult to get a handle on. A thorough presentation of strengths and deficiencies may be the best way to a sound decision. The board might appoint a committee of school personnel, with or without outside members, to present all aspects of a question.

But when an issue is controversial, the use of an in-house committee should be handled carefully. Unfortunately, this is often not the case. I've seen boards, with a hot potato on their hands, ask the superintendent to have a committee study the matter and recommend a course of action. Often, this is simply a delaying action, deferring a tough decision to a later time.

Once the committee does what it was asked to do, sometimes after much toil and deliberation, the board finally bites the bullet. It struggles to a decision, and then may well reject the committee's report. This is simply bad administrative procedure. I'm not saying the board should automatically accept other people's work. This would in effect yield its decision-making responsibility to another body. Instead, I'm saying that a committee should be asked merely to obtain the information the board needs. Only after a decision has been made should a group be charged with fleshing out the details of its implementation.

If a report is rejected, the committee members, who usually have come to believe in their ideas, sometimes passionately, often feel not only that their time has been wasted, but that they're being told their thinking is unacceptable. This is damaging to morale.

I have great admiration for school boards and the people who serve on them, and I hope nothing I've said will be construed as criticism. I won't say anything about extreme situations which occasionally arise, and create problems for everyone concerned—circumstances like a board which basically represents only one side of a deeply divided community, or one deadlocked within itself, or at loggerheads with its own superintendent. Fortunately, such cases are rare. When they do occur, each community must deal with the situation in its own way.

A board should look at its practices from time to time. Like everyone else, members can benefit from feedback telling them how others feel affected by their decisions. They might wish to commission a study to identify various ways of developing consensus in conflicted areas, with the possible reward of obtaining useful ideas.

Possible studies and activities: Here are some suggestions for ways to look at the organization of the school system:

Examine mathematics, and ask the teachers to state if the subject would benefit from a change in organization or time allotted.

Ask the same question about class size, length of sessions, and/or number of sessions a week.

Create a schedule reflecting answers to the above.

Survey a school building, to decide the changes that would be needed to do any of the above.

Look at districts which grant some degree of autonomy to individual schools, to identify strengths and weaknesses.

Experiment by giving a school limited curricular autonomy, and evaluating results.

Do a cost-benefit study of procedures used for district-wide coordination and communication.

Do a cost-benefit study of the use of outside consultants.

Experiment to find the best way to use a committee for research and planning.

19. The teaching profession

The teaching profession is constantly under attack. Indeed, many don't even think it's a profession at all. There's the old saying, "Those who can, ...do; those who can't, ...teach"?

Almost every aspect of education is questioned: 1) the selection of teachers, 2) their preparation, 3) education as a discipline ("college politics"), 4) admission into the profession, 5) professional standards. I'll address all of these.

The selection of teachers. Critics often say that too many students with marginal GPA's enter teacher-education programs. They ask why the profession can't attract candidates who are more outstanding. Perhaps this is not so surprising, though, when comments like the one above are commonplace.

Many countries attract higher-caliber teaching prospects than the U.S. Japan and Finland are two examples. Perhaps this is because they have such high regard for teachers. In Japan, for example, all you have to do is say that you're a teacher to receive the deepest of bows. In Finland, so many highly talented students apply that only a small fraction is accepted.

I'm not sure why Americans hold teaching in such low esteem. Possibly, it's because so many academicians disrespect it as a discipline, and deride it. Or, it may stem from the value we've historically placed on "can-do" work. In any event, it's unfortunate that teachers often have to prove their worth to doubting parents. It certainly makes it hard to attract people to the profession.

Suggestions have been made that we offer better pay, in order to attract abler people. But there's no certainty this would work. High-ability persons could probably command similar, or even higher, salaries elsewhere, and the effort might result mainly in attracting additional applicants from among people who might otherwise settle for poorer-paid jobs.

It's also been suggested that a high GPA be required for admission to a teacher-education program. But, aside from the fact that this might reduce the number of applicants, the unfortunate truth is that high grades are not always a warranty of teaching success. I knew a man with a Ph.D. in Physics who volunteered to teach at the local secondary school. His offer was accepted gratefully by the superintendent, who pressured the State Department of Education to issue him an emergency certificate. But he had to be uninvited after one semester because no one in his class understood what he was talking about.

I have no argument with the need for teachers to know their subject well. Although I do have a story to tell. My very first job was overseas in an American school. I had been hired at long distance as a teacher of mathematics, my college major, by the school's director, who thought he'd specified math and physics in his written offer. When I convinced him that his letter had failed to do this, he asked in a very small voice, "You can teach physics, can't you?" Since it was much too late to get anyone else, I said I'd try, although my total background in the subject was a high-school course in physics and a college course in mechanics.

A funny thing happened. I taught physics better than I taught any of my math classes. I knew the latter subject backwards and forwards, while in physics I had to learn as I went along, together with the class. Any qualified science major would not have made the mistakes I made. But maybe also might not have done some of the things I did right. I was so attuned to the class' needs, since I shared their difficulties, that I made certain that once we'd finished a topic, they really knew it. I almost lost my math students, though, because I expected too much, and couldn't see why they didn't understand.

I certainly don't recommend that anyone teach a subject he or she doesn't know well. But this incident taught me how important it is for a teacher to ensure that students understand, and ascertain what troubles they're having, and why. Skilled teaching truly requires instructional skills, and admission to a teacher-education program needs more evidence than a simple grade-point average. I certainly believe that teachers should possess subject-matter mastery, but I don't want anyone to teach who can't find out why students are not learning, or who doesn't care.

So, in addition to using academic achievement as a prerequisite for entering the teaching profession, we need additional criteria. What might these be? And how can we get them? They must be based on how we define teaching. Besides subject-matter competence, it involves the ability to manage a class full of students at various levels of ability and attainment. It's also requires the skill and the willingness to engage in effective two-way communication between instructor and learner. To say nothing of the mastery of instruments and procedures of evaluation. To me, there truly is a discipline of education. I'll discuss this issue later.

How do we select persons who can do these things? This question has baffled educators for years, since oftentimes, efforts to develop these talents have foundered on recipients' reluctance to use them. I've seen many prospective teachers demonstrate knowledge of procedures in college which they fail to use later. Apparently, there's some element of personality which affects an individual's classroom procedures. We need to study this matter, and identify the kind of person who possesses what I'll call a predisposition to be a teacher-mentor.

There's no doubt we need to get the best people possible. There's also no doubt that we need to look at personality, as well as academics. Some colleges are trying to do this. But we need to do more. And we certainly need to find ways to make the profession more attractive.

The preparation of teachers. When we do get applicants, how do we prepare them to be teachers? There's much criticism of present college programs. Many former students are frank to say they don't feel the courses they took helped them very much. Critics add that a major reason able students avoid the profession is their reluctance to subject themselves to dreary programs.

Critics also note that many persons who haven't participated in formal teacher preparation have taught successfully. They point to non-certified teachers in private or church schools as evidence that it's not necessary. Perhaps it's evidence of the predisposition I've just mentioned. Many projects have been developed recently, to enable college graduates without formal preparation to teach while learning on the job. Doubtless, this attracts motivated people, and if successful, is worth wider use. I'll discuss this activity later.

I'd like to look, though, at two specific aspects of formal teacher education. The first is what courses and experiences are prescribed. The second is how these are conducted. I spent most of my career as a professor of education, and must confess I don't think I was as successful as I wished. So who am I to say what should be done? All I can do is report what I observed.

Much of my work in education was in Colorado, and I'll use it as an example. Every institution of higher education has its own, supposedly unique, teacher-training program. And I've seen none that was developed on any other basis than the faculty's considered judgment. The resulting proposal was presented to the State Department of Education, and, possibly after discussion and revision, approved as fulfilling certification requirements. Multiply the number of colleges in Colorado by fifty and you have some picture of the multiplicity of endeavors on American campuses.

In most colleges and universities, responsibility for the preparation of teachers is shared by the department (or school or college) of education and various subject-matter departments, frequently with little coordination among them. I'll discuss this in my next section, when I examine campus politics. Most institutions don't offer a major in education, except possibly in elementary education, and sometimes not then.

Subject-matter competence is stressed for all teacher-trainees. Those at the secondary level must major in at least one of the fields they'll serve. If they aspire to two fields, they need considerable extra work in the second. The future elementary teacher is expected to take courses in several disciplines. These requirements have tended to increase over the years.

Almost all teacher education programs share three basic elements: 1) courses which provide background learning believed to be essential for teachers, 2) methods courses, which focus on classroom techniques, and 3) field work in off-campus classrooms. Plus the subject-matter requirements I've already mentioned. I believe there are a number of problems.

I'll start with background learnings. These are education courses heavily reliant on such fields as psychology, philosophy, sociology, and history. In my day, they had titles like "The American Public School" or "Foundations of Education." Today, they have evolved, and bear more sophisticated names like "School and Society" or "Human Growth and Development." They represent broad sweeps of information about education and the factors and forces which relate to it. They're often taught without any apparent relationship to what goes on in a classroom, at least in the minds of students in them. To me, they belong more in the subject field to which they're indebted than in teacher education.

We haven't really listened to our students, and our former students, when they complain that such courses are dull, boring, and of little use to them. Faculties have justified them by saying that teachers need breadth of background, and of course they do. But beginners don't see that need. They want specifics to help them get started. And since the courses frequently appear near the start of the program of preparation, students have no frame of reference to help them appreciate the need for background. This reverses the best learning process, since generalized learnings come before specific ones, instead of the reverse. And it's not only beginners who don't see their value; many experienced teachers don't either.

There seems to be a trend toward less emphasis on this type of course, which to me often looked more like social science than preparation for the classroom. (I never saw any research evidence showing that they affected future teaching performance.) There's a growing focus on more practical matters, with ever-increasing use of field observation or participation, commonly in conjunction with a class taught on campus. Many of these offerings require students to spend extensive time in outside schoolrooms, observing teachers and students in action, and contributing appropriately as requested.

Then, there are the methods courses. Presumably, these focus on the best techniques for helping students learn a subject. On most campuses, they are controlled by the subject-matter faculty. The rationale for this is that only those who are thoroughly grounded in a subject can teach it well, and professors in that field are the best grounded. The result often is that students try to teach the way their professors taught them. More about this later.

Finally, there's student-teaching—sometimes called by names like practicum or internship—where trainees are responsible for existing classrooms in schools under the supervision of experienced teachers. This is the capstone of teacher preparation, and is subject to many problems.

First and foremost is the quality of the supervising teacher. Presumably, only the best teachers in a school are called upon to supervise neophytes. In practice, though, many of these don't want to be called on repeatedly, and others in the school seek the prestige of being selected. So, there's a possibility that a supervising teacher is not always the best.

Presumably, the education professor overseeing the student-teacher controls this with the power to approve or disapprove a principal's selection. But again, other considerations may be in play. Colleges are often loath to risk their good relationship with a school by overruling a principal. Generally, the professor does not know the faculty well enough, and must depend on the principal's judgment.

In any event, the future teacher is greatly influenced by the supervising teacher's methods. Indeed, the way that the latter teaches, and the way the methods teacher teaches, and the techniques subject-matter professors use, influence a beginning teacher more than anything any education professor says or does.

There's an additional difficulty with student-teaching. That is how a grade is assigned. Practices vary. Sometimes, the supervising teacher assigns the grade. This is often permitted to express the college's confidence in the experienced teacher and to maintain good relations. This is O.K. if there's absolute confidence in this individual. But at the very least, the college has surrendered its responsibility to someone outside it.

Sometimes the college professor gives the grade, but this is certainly based on less frequent observation of the student than the supervising teacher has made. It has the same weakness as a principal's evaluation of a faculty member based on a limited number of observations.

Sometimes, it is done jointly by the two people involved, although this can be a problem if either one feels strongly. And the task is further complicated by the fact that supervising teachers may vary widely in the standards to which they hold student-teachers.

And now to look at my second area of concern—how well teacher education programs are conducted. Aren't prospective teachers, perhaps for the first time in their lives, studying their own teachers, and using this observation to help them decide how they themselves should teach? At this critical juncture, the teachers they observe are mostly college professors. Since they're often taught through lectures, it's easy for them to conclude that lecturing is the essence of teaching, even though some subjects, like music and drama, are performance-oriented.

Unfortunately, much of the teaching by the education faculty relies on lecturing, especially in the broad background courses which have received so many complaints. Why is it done this way? If education professors believe good classroom techniques are vital, why don't they use them? Instead it's often, "Do as I say, don't do as I do."

Before I began to teach at the college level, I'd come to use much hands-on learning and small-group work in my math classroom. But once I became a professor, I largely reverted to lecturing. And I saw other faculty members doing the same. Today, I can't believe we all thought we'd encourage future teachers to address individual differences without doing more of it ourselves.

In the later years of my college teaching, I'd begun to experiment with student participation, both in planning and evaluation. And I recall times when I encouraged student activity in the classroom— moments when they were learning by "doing." But I fear it was too little, too late, and I did much too much "telling." I can see why folks say hindsight is 20-20. I do believe it's more like 40-20.

Why do education professors lecture so much? Perhaps because they were taught that way themselves. It might be the weight of tradition. Or it's just the easy way out. Maybe they aren't thinking clearly, or the crush of daily pressures doesn't give them time to think. Whatever the reason, it was wrong when I was active, and it's still wrong today.

How are methods classes taught? Too often, mainly through lectures. After all, many if not most of them are conducted by subject-matter specialists. Little attention is paid to individualization of instruction, classroom organization, or (often) how to construct and analyze tests. They tend to focus on clear presentation of the subject, with little concern about finding out why some students don't learn.

But education professors are on uncertain ground if they complain about this, since their own practices are suspect. They shouldn't be surprised that students look elsewhere to model their efforts. Nor wonder why they hear them say education courses are not helpful.

Much of what I've said about the high-school curriculum applies here. Every part of a teacher-education program should show a demonstrable influence on future performance. It's not enough to say, "All teachers should know this or that." Why should they? If it's to affect their professional work, show the evidence that it does. If you can't, replace it with something which can show evidence. We mustn't allow our programs to drive away well-qualified persons.

We need many improvements, including better methods courses and student-teaching experiences. We need to look at new practices, like on-the-job training, apprenticeships and internships. Let's find the elements of preparation which correlate with instructional success, to ensure that certification truly distinguishes between qualified and unqualified individuals.

Education as a discipline. College academicians are part of the teaching profession, even if they deny it themselves. They think of themselves as dedicated primarily to a subject field, and its furtherance through study and transmission. But this transmission is an act of instruction. And if they teach methods courses, they are presumably training people to be successful instructors. They must be considered to be teacher educators. Many of them, though, not only disdain education as a discipline, they are sometimes even indifferent to learners.

An associate professor of sociology once said to me, "I couldn't care less what my students think of me. My job is to present the subject. Theirs is to learn it." This was after her dean had inaugurated a program asking students to rate their teachers anonymously, and had charged the Bureau of Educational Research, of which I was a part, with the responsibility of collecting the information and reporting it to the faculty involved. She refused even to look at the data we had collected.

I often encountered this attitude among academicians, although rarely to this extent. Still, their attitude often was that subject-matter comes first and the student comes second, as proclaimed by the Arts and Sciences dean I described earlier. Yet, from these ranks come most teachers of methods courses.

Now I must admit I have an ax to grind. I was a professor of education, with an Ed. D. degree, and acutely aware that many fellow faculty members considered my field to be at best a second-rate discipline. I think I can safely describe their position as the conviction that anyone well grounded in a subject is able to teach it without requiring anything taught in education courses. (Could the Ph.D. in physics, who couldn't succeed in high school, have been an exception?)

I'll tell a story. When I was a professor at the Graduate School of Education at Rutgers University, I learned that some faculty members of the College of Arts and Sciences were preparing a petition to submit to state authorities. It called for the abolition of the school where I was teaching, on the grounds that education was not a discipline worthy of a distinguished university. The petition got nowhere, but you see my point.

So you can see that I wrestled throughout my career with the feeling that academicians didn't care as much about learners as I did, and didn't respect what I tried to do. I realize that this is unfair to many open-minded colleagues, and to many supremely talented college teachers, some of whom I took courses from. I'll try to be as evenhanded as possible in my further observations of professorial stands and college politics.

What is a discipline? Dictionary definitions are not very helpful, so I'll try my own. I'll call it a body of knowledge and understandings related a common focus, with procedures and generalizations which can be tested by research. Many academicians consider education not to be a discipline because they don't see much more involved than presenting the subject, à la the sociology professor. This is the disconnect between the education faculty and others. Yet it is from the latter that methods-course instructors are frequently drawn. It's no wonder many neophyte teachers do much lecturing.

I believe the field of education is a legitimate discipline. I've already listed several areas which must be mastered and procedures which must be learned. There's need to know the various ways people learn, and how group structure and dynamics affect classroom effectiveness. Teachers need skills in counseling and observation, they should have speech training, and the ability to use many different classroom techniques, like various ways to organize it for different purposes. What about the ability to diagnose students' differing needs and interests?

Now please bear with me briefly while I consider "college politics." I almost called this section of the book by that name, because we see so much contention and conflict on campuses.

The faculty of an institution of higher education basically controls the curriculum. In consequence, there's a temptation to consider all proposals for change in terms of how they affect one's department. If its course load is materially increased or diminished, a change can have a major impact. This explains much of the controversy about teacher education programs, with professors on both sides of the question defending their turf—education faculty no less vigorously than academicians. You can see the maelstrom of emotions I referred to earlier, within which all educational planners must function. It seems remarkably difficult for highly-educated individuals, all dedicated to searching for truth in their own fields of concern, to reach a meeting of minds.

I'm going to tell another story. Or two. In my final college job, I was chairman of the committee empowered to approve or disapprove students for admission to the teacher-education program. Frequently, the academic advisor of a marginal candidate would ask that the candidate be given benefit of the doubt. Other committee members sometimes took the position that the candidate's future students should receive this benefit. The matter was usually settled by a straight vote, with neither side making a real effort to achieve consensus. This is the disconnect I just mentioned.

At another time in the same institution, the Department of Education made a proposal for a new program leading to a Master of Arts in Teaching. This was developed because the department felt there was not enough space in the undergraduate curriculum to teach all the skills the faculty thought future teachers needed. I might add that the institution had no major in education, even for future elementary-school teachers. Everyone had to have a subject major. In consequence, there was a squeeze in education courses because so much else was required. The new program was designed to provide additional professionalized learning.

But when the program was presented to the entire faculty, various subject-matter departments united in insisting that it should include additional requirements in their own field. In the end, the M.A.T. program was almost half composed of subject-matter specifications. Apparently, some professors believed that possession of an undergraduate major was no longer sufficient preparation for a school teacher.

The strong tendency for professors to take positions on issues based more upon the needs of their own department than on what is best for the institution is what I mean by college politics. It makes curricular changes very difficult.

I do not say, or believe, that education professors are right and others are wrong. But I do want to show how fiercely faculty members defend their specialties. Yet we must find a way to resolve such conflicts through reason and restraint. There's much research in existence about how to do group planning and reach consensus. Colleges should be more open to applying what we already know.

Unfortunately, many of the departments where such research is done do not possess the high regard of the arts and sciences.

All professors are truly members of the teaching profession. Their institutions are a vital part of the nation's overall plan for preparing young people for life. Like the elementary and secondary schools, they should seek evidence regarding the effectiveness of their programs and practices, and should not assume they already have the answers. I hope college faculty members can be as open to objective studies examining curricular and instructional effectiveness as they are to research in their own disciplines.

Entering the profession. Most teachers enter the profession by receiving certification, sometimes called licensure. It means the state attests he or she is qualified to teach, and it's typically granted to individuals who've successfully completed an approved program of preparation. But, as I've said, these programs vary widely, even within a single state.

Certification should mean we know what knowledge and skills a teacher needs to possess, and we've made sure new teachers have acquired them. But have we? I've presented evidence that we don't, especially given the success of so many non-certificated individuals. There must be one or more factors involved in instructional competence that are not considered in certification.

For lack of a better thought, let me assume there's some element in a person's makeup that enables him or her to teach well. We need to determine this quality and find ways to identify it in an individual. Doing so could make our programs of preparation more successful.

In addition to teachers who don't seem to need training, there are others who don't seem to benefit from it. They can pass courses, and follow directions, apparently without internalizing their learning. I've known teachers who don't get better with experience, and who don't return from advanced degrees with noticeable improvement. Possibly they lack this quality.

I'm not saying experience and degrees are not valuable. I do say that their benefits are not automatic. A good teacher gets better by acquiring new information and skills. Non-certificated people already teaching successfully are no exception. Undoubtedly there are things they don't know.

We should welcome the experimental programs that permit able college graduates without certification to get on-the-job training under supervision. Often, these have attracted highly-motivated people who provide desperately-needed help at inner-city schools. It will help us if we study them, as well as successful non-certificated teachers. We might identify the quality that seems to elude us.

In-service education of teachers. This is a catchall term that covers almost anything a school does to help teachers improve. It appears almost everywhere, in various forms and with varying degrees of success. Because of this variance, it sorely needs reexamination.

The basic concept behind in-service education is that everyone can benefit from exposure to new ideas, and all schools will get better as their teachers get better. Practically, though, it runs into all kinds of difficulties, not the least of which is people's widespread aversion to being told what to do. School leaders maintain that this is not what in-service programs do, that they merely provide opportunities for teachers to learn what the teachers themselves feel they need to know.

There's no doubt that if this condition prevails, in-service education is of much value. Often, though, it does not. I've seen sessions where teachers sit with arms crossed, as if daring someone to say something they might accept.

Earlier, I considered ways in which principals and supervisors might foster change without arousing resistance. Later, in Chapter 9, I discussed resistance further. So I won't repeat myself here. Yet, this is the challenge. Unless and until teachers see a need for change, very little is going to occur, regardless of how well the in-service program is explained, justified, or conducted. It's vital that their interests and concerns be addressed in a manner they view as helpful, and not as directive.

But there are other issues too. The leader of any in-service program must be skillful in adapting it to the actual needs of the teachers in the specific school situation. They should avoid the mistakes of overgeneralizing and over-presentation that college instructors have been known to make. They must not seem to be teaching a college course or any part of one.

Unless, of course, the in-service program is openly conducted for college credit, and can be used toward the acquisition of a degree in an institution of the participant's choosing. This is very sticky, however. It requires joint planning by school authorities and college faculties, and should not require participants to pay tuition. I have not seen it used widely.

Still, despite the difficulties I've cited, the importance of in-service education should not be underestimated. As I've said, we all need to learn and grow, and if a school can generate open-mindedness and receptivity in teachers, it will benefit hugely from any programs which ensue.

Standards of the profession. We all think we know what high standards mean. But do we? This is another catchall heading, covering a multitude of areas: student performance, evaluation of instruction, teachers' unions, teacher-education programs, state government, testing programs, and more. Everyone has an opinion, and they often conflict—sometimes vehemently.

Central to all of them though is how an instructor performs. Every suggestion for raising standards is devoted in some way or other to the improvement of students' learning. And the key to that is the teacher in the classroom.

So every proposal for improvements must be justified by this criterion first and foremost. Much dispute might be avoided if, instead of arguing the relative merits of one procedure or another, we go back to basics and ask how each might benefit learners, and enable teachers to more effective.

And if every change, or even a large minority, leads better learning, there is no limit to the level of the standards we can aspire to.

Possible studies and activities

Develop additional criteria to use with the GPA for admission to a teacher-training program.

Compare students' later teaching practices with what they were taught regarding classroom procedures.

Canvass professors who are teaching education and methods courses about the use of individualized instruction in their classes.

Find places where longer internships or on-the-job training are taking place, to identify their successes and difficulties.

Devise a list of the elements of good teaching which could be objectively observed or otherwise assessed.

Locate schools using evaluation of instruction as a basis for merit pay, to find how successful and well-received it is.

Do likewise with districts who've made modifications in teacher tenure policies.

Similarly with the use of teachers to evaluate instruction and make recommendations.

20. Expectations

Why do I include this section when discussing things that need change? Do I really think educators can change the expectations of employers, colleges, parents, or the community? No, I don't. At least, not very much. But everything changes over time, and I'd like to consider it here.

The only way for schools to influence expectations is with concrete evidence, and it's not easy even then. Humans are notoriously unwilling to change their minds, especially when they feel strongly. Many present school practices induce that response.

The schools are well aware of this, and have adapted to reality. But I have two points to make. The first is that if educators disagree with anyone's expectations, they have a professional obligation to say so. It should be done without confrontation, demands, or unilateral action, and accompanied by information which supports their views. If consensus can't be reached, efforts should be redoubled to do research and increase participation. Only as a last resort should school authorities make decisions without community support.

My second point is that educators need to be aware of changes which might have taken place without their knowing. For instance, college requirements have quietly become more general, and less specific. Employers place greater emphasis on social skills. Such events have implications for schools, but won't influence anything unless educators are sensitive to them.

The expectations which have most affected the schools are probably those of colleges. But the Eight-Year Study showed that these didn't have to dominate the curriculum, and institutions of higher education might be amenable to change. Thoughtful efforts to find new and better forms of secondary education might have at least a chance of changing expectations.

But if schools are faced with an overwhelming abundance of expectations, and it's not possible to meet them all, what should be done, and by whom? For example, if high schools should make college prep courses elective, and this does not accord with college expectations, who should give way? Since school programs exist to fulfill the expectations of the community, colleges would have to adapt.

I'm profoundly convinced that our schools belong to us, the nation's citizens. If their main expectations are for public education to produce fully functioning members of society, then that becomes the schools' highest priority. Every other outcome, and I do mean every other one, is secondary in importance.

I know I've said all this before. But I don't feel the man on the street and the parent in the parlor totally realize it. The schools exist to educate our children, and the best way to do it should shape everyone's expectations and not the other way around. Unless an expectation is universal. If colleges and employers can be persuaded that well-rounded individuals will perform better in their establishments, they might I accept a new approach as being of value to them. If they do, parents and citizens would too.

Possible studies and activities:

Survey the entrance requirements of a number of institutions of higher education to see exactly what they are and how much they vary.

Canvass a number of employers of various types and sizes, asking what they look for in candidates for jobs.

Contact parents in various minority groups, asking what they expect the schools to do for their children.

Do likewise with a sample of parents of students who qualify for a free lunch program.

Encourage the community to develop a mission statement for their schools, or restudy one which already exists.

Examine your school's present program, to determine where it reflects any of the foregoing findings and where it doesn't.

PART SIX

A Better School System

IT'S GOING TO BE DIFFICULT FOR ME TO SAY MUCH MORE. I'M REMINDED of the churchgoer who remarked after the pastor had produced an exceedingly long sermon, "He sure missed a lot of good chances to stop."

Perhaps I'm doing the same. Still, I'd like to end this little volume with a vision of what the education of tomorrow could be like. And I'm talking about a tomorrow I shall never live to see, and perhaps you won't either.

I've said what I think should be changed, and frequently what I believe the changes should be. So what more is there? Basically, it's to remind us of the three major challenges American schools face, not always successfully. They'll still face them in the future. The three are: 1) fulfilling the wishes of the community, 2) meeting the needs of the students, and 3) meeting the needs of the nation.

In my remaining remarks, I'll not say anything I haven't said already. Still, I want to put them in an organized pattern together. And I'm going to replace statements that we should do this or that with the overoptimistic, "We will do this or that."

21. Fulfilling the wishes of the community

Local control of education has proven its superiority to centralized administration, and will continue to be the standard. But since the schools cannot vary greatly from community desires, there will be an established structure for two-way communication between the citizenry and the decision-makers. The process will be improved and systematized beyond elections, public meetings, petitions, and various forms of protest. In this way, authorities will be apprised of any shifts in community thinking. Which will not only assist the board, but diminish the likelihood of unexpected criticisms and demands. How it will be done may vary from place to place, but it will be done.

The school board is usually composed of part-time volunteers with full-time work responsibilities elsewhere, and often has too much to do. They need the best, and the most reliable, information they can get. Procedures will be established for providing this. They'll receive up-to-date information about promising educational practices, wherever they occur. They'll have comprehensive information about the pro's and con's of any major policy issue. This will go beyond a simple request to the superintendent, or other local professional staff, to furnish it.

These two practices will help board members increase their confidence and comfort when establishing policies and approving programs.

22. Meeting the needs of the students

The schools of the future will show a marked improvement over those of today, They'll place a higher priority on meeting all needs of all students. At present, we may not even have met all the needs of any one.

The following outcomes will be accepted as desirable for every graduate. These represent the essentials necessary for young men and women to enter society as fully-functioning adults

All who complete the twelfth grade will be able:

1. To communicate effectively through speaking and writing.

2. To do critical thinking and use evidence to make choices.

3. To practice the habits of good health.

4. To acquire and maintain strong human relationships.

5. To function successfully in a field of work.

6. To be a useful and active citizen.

7. To deal successfully with the common tasks of everyday life.

Every area of study required by the schools will be judged in terms of its role in furthering one or more of the above. If not essential for this purpose, it will be elective.

In addition, all graduates will demonstrate:

1. Strong moral values,

2. A love of learning.

3. Realistic and comprehensive self-awareness.

4. Sensitivity to the needs and wishes of others.

Schools will examine their practices regularly to ensure that:

1. Desired outcomes are described so clearly that teachers' responsibilities are obvious, and evaluation instruments can be created.

2. Student achievement toward all outcomes is measured, recorded, and reported. The failing grade has been replaced with a record of what the student has actually accomplished. The ABCDF grading system is replaced with a procedure for providing detailed, specific information about student achievement.

3. The needs of sub-groupings of students {ethnic, racial, socio-economic, capability, etc.) are identified, planned for, and addressed.

4. The essential instructional emphasis will be upon learning by doing, instead of learning by listening.

5. Students with handicaps, deficiencies, or other special needs will be given special attention.

Schools and districts will be smaller, and schools within a large district given program autonomy. In large schools which still exist, the student body will be divided into groups, like schools within a school, in order to provide the benefits of greater student participation and closer relationships between teachers and students.

To sum up, tomorrow's schools will have a wide variety of learning experiences for students with a wide variety of learning needs. They'll have a planned, concerted effort to emphasize all educational outcomes, with an array of measuring instruments, and a program for recording and reporting all accomplishments of all students.

23. Meeting the needs of the nation

Finally, how will we meet the needs of the nation? Local control of education creates a major challenge—how to obtain appropriate coordination among countless districts and independent schools. A second problem is how to reach consensus about national needs in the midst of an array of counteracting forces—fifty legislatures, governors, commissioners of education, the U.S. Congress, countless lobbyists, and many impassioned special-interest groups. A third is how to ensure federal and state initiatives don't impinge on local prerogatives.

There are parallels between reaching agreement locally and reaching it nationally. Both require regular and systematic two-way communication and the best information available. But the intensity of disagreement and the virulence in Washington, to say nothing about the huge financial forces, dwarf what we normally witness in communities. I'm not as confident about predicting on a country-wide basis as I am locally. So I'll stop using the future tense, and turn back to that old standby, "should."

Many organizations are now trying to improve communication and spread authentic information nationally—associations of governors and other state leaders, clusters of professional specialists, and groups focusing on special needs. But the widespread suspicion that they have axes to grind interfere with their effectiveness. We must find a way to dispel unwarranted mistrust. Perhaps our polling systems can play a role in this. I'm convinced that constant distribution of unbiased information and presence of channels of communication will yield less conflict and controversy, and fewer stubborn standoffs.

We need at least three efforts:

1. Creation of a reliable means to distinguish between authentic information and that provided by single-focus advocates.

2. A procedure for distributing this authentic information to all in a position to take action.

3. Studies by carefully-selected groups on how government needs should affect schools, and legislative bodies can best interact with local educational authorities.

Legislators and government officials should resist the huge temptation to believe they "know best," and have a responsibility to ensure compliance by passing laws and dispensing funds. Instead, their actions should reflect the best practices, the best professional thought, and the best evidence of citizens' consensus. Pressure from any source should be tested against this consensus.

Still, regardless of the issues that consume Washington at any given moment, the nation will always need leaders. It will also need productive workers, effective family members, concerned citizens, and persons who fit well into society. But these are also the priorities of all schools, or should be. Working on them locally will serve the U.S. The nation needs all this, and probably much more. But it will always benefit if young people become the best they can be.

In a word, people should find ways to work together, and rein in the excesses of advocacy. Once consensus about the nation's needs is reached, the schools will know what to do.

I'm well aware that I've proposed far more than can be realistically expected. But, as Browning wrote, "....a man's reach must exceed his grasp, or what's a heaven for?" We must strive endlessly, be grateful for what we achieve, and never cease to reach for more.

A Case Study: Critical Thinking

THE PURPOSE OF THIS APPENDIX IS TO PROVIDE AN ILLUSTRATION OF how an individual educator, or a small group of them, might realistically undertake a study. I make the assumption that no one involved has had specialized training in research or evaluation, and no helpers with such background are available. In brief, I want action research done.

Action research. What is that? It's a concept which had a short active life in the 1950's. I was impressed by its relevance then, and feel it is no less relevant today. And a glance at the internet shows signs of continuing interest.

Basically, it relies on the idea that those who work most closely with learners on an everyday basis represent an immense resource for studying how to educate them better. Their firsthand knowledge of their students and their intense concern for them represent a valuable resource. The challenge is how to marshal this force and focus its efforts. Many would call it simply an attempt to put a respectable face on trial and error.

Many extensive definitions of action research were proposed at one time, some of them quite elaborate, with specific suggestions for improving participants' investigative abilities. However, the approach didn't resonate widely within the profession, and the concept went into limbo as a result.

But I still think the immensity of the resource means a way must be found to use it for research, and this is what I wish to discuss. I have the feeling that the very mass of many findings by many teachers, if these are in basic agreement, surely is a powerful learning. And we have seen evidence of this in recent years in the rise of what is called meta-analysis, where a large number of findings from various places, obtained in various ways and with various levels of expertise, are reviewed in assemblage, to see if worthwhile generalizations emerge. This is the approach I'm suggesting.

When a sizable number of teachers, with all kinds of backgrounds, abilities, and interests, all make efforts to improve some aspect of education, any area of general agreement they reach must surely be of value, and should receive widespread consideration. All that is needed to accomplish this is their willingness to try something new, open-mindedness about results, and use of common sense and their best professional judgment. If they should strive to improve their research knowledge and skills so much the better, but I wouldn't expect it.

The action-research approach foundered so many years ago because its enthusiasts were high on the thought that teachers would acquire all kinds of new skills. And the teachers didn't buy that. Let's hope I do better. I won't make proposals for how teachers might change. Rather, I suggest a simpler approach to the whole concept of research.

We tend to think of it in terms of standards. We devise new and better ways to observe, to evaluate, and to design experiments—all with the thought in mind of improving the degree of confidence we have in our findings. One consequence of this is that it becomes harder and harder to find persons with the necessary skills, and when we do find them, they are frequently far removed from the everyday realities of the classroom. Often, they have difficulty explaining to teachers what it is they're trying to do, while the latter may fail to make all their concerns and insights available to the specialists. To say nothing about the fact researchers have been known to condescend to field workers.

I add this appendix because I want to show how challenges of innovation can be faced in real life. I sought to do what I ask you to do. I took an objective, and used it for planning a study and preparing its evaluation. I tried to be quite specific, defining outcomes behaviorally, and seeking ways to assess achievement and report results.

About this study. Basically, most educational progress, and indeed, all research proceeds in the same way. We get ideas from experience or study. We try promising ones to see if they work. We evaluate the results, and sooner or later, find we've gained ground. It really is just a careful form of trial-and-error.

Any effort to innovate is a leap in the dark. And when I started to consider a study about critical thinking, I wasn't sure I'd arrive at a useful ending. Now that I'm through, I'm still not sure. I leave you to judge, but still hope my leaping will help you. I made a commitment to myself not to hide anything and not to second-guess. I believe I kept it, and didn't try to "improve" on first efforts. There was no rewriting.

(Author's note: I really mean what I just said. I report exactly what I did to plan and work on the study, including all fumbles and missteps. I tried to do it the same way that teachers without special training would proceed—without specialized assistance and with only their own experience and common sense to make decisions. The only time previously that I myself had ever done anything about critical thinking was years ago in my doctoral program, when I made a critique of the tests which had been published on the topic. They only thing I remember learning is that everyone had a different definition.)

I describe all steps, problems, uncertainties, confusions, and doubts, because I suspect many others might have the same difficulties if making a similar effort. And I detail results, without any claim of success. Only by being brutally honest can I have any influence and persuade you to try something you doubt your ability to do. Or cheer you up if you're already struggling.

At the end of this report there's a critique. This really is second-guessing. It's what I conclude upon reviewing the efforts I made. I try to identify what could and should have been done better, or differently. I hope it gives you a basis to critique your own efforts and benefit from your mistakes. I've also added some notes in italics throughout the original account, to show how certain choices could or should have been improved. These are of course afterthoughts, added after the study was finished. In what now follows, I shall use the present tense to report the past, since I want you to feel the same immediacy as I did while I was proceeding.

Why "critical thinking"? Well, I have to start somewhere. If the essence of innovation is looking at a new and different objective, or a new way to tackle an old one, the first step is selecting the objective on which to focus. I don't want to use any of the standard subject-matter objectives, and I don't want to stray too far into areas of values and habits, mainly because I don't want to start out by losing everyone who rejects such areas as not being the business of the schools.

Critical thinking seems to fill the bill. Clearly related to the intellect, it seems vital to much subject-matter learning. And it's also widely viewed as a desirable for citizens, and especially workers. It has the further value that it's not well understood, so it presents a challenge in reaching consensus.

I've already reported that fifty years ago, I saw no evidence of agreement. I say the same thing today. In that survey long ago, I found, somewhat to my surprise, that every test seemed to be measuring something different from every other, although they all had "critical thinking" in their title.

After all these years, I'm no longer sure what I found, although I do recall that one test focused on study skills, another, numerical problems, and a third had logic challenges like those now seen in puzzle books. All were different.

Creating a definition. Looking up definitions in the dictionary or encyclopedia is a waste of time. They're much too general. Encarta calls critical thinking "disciplined intellectual criticism that combines research, knowledge of historical context, and balanced judgment." Wikipedia says it's a process "....that questions assumptions....and (is) a way of deciding whether a claim is true, false, sometimes true, or partly true." How different these are. And how non-specific. What I said in Chapter 14 about "Goals for Education in Colorado" certainly applies here.

I think I shouldn't continue searching for an acceptable definition in books—for two reasons. First, I doubt if I can find any consensus. Second, I feel that that even if I get one, it won't be useful.

Maybe I should have searched further.

It won't be useful because teachers who try to help students learn to think critically have their own ideas. This is not to say that field workers know better than scholars. Rather, it says that those who seek an educational outcome have to right to decide what it is they're working toward, and have a right to name it. If it appears to be a careful thought process, is acceptable to the community, and if they wish to call it critical thinking, then it is critical thinking, at least for one school. Experts may say it's incorrectly named, but whether it is or is not, it's the objective desired.

Now I have the task of creating a definition. I feel uncomfortable doing this. Isn't it presumptuous for me to define a term which is so widely respected, even if it doesn't enjoy unity of opinion? Yet it might be easier to get agreement from a group of teachers based on their personal experience than from a gaggle of intellectuals concerned with generalizations.

Perhaps I might have started out without a prior decision as to what it was I was looking for, but rather to have begun by seeking behaviors generally seen as desirable in students, such as good thinking habits. What we end up with could be named later.

One thing that comforts me is that whatever specific definition is acquired, it will almost certainly be an outcome most people would see as valuable. Even if specific behaviors implied by one definition differ from those implied by another, the behaviors are probably all desirable. The goals of education are so encompassing that they contain vast numbers of specific worthwhile behaviors. So, I shall go ahead with my own definition, knowing it may not be supported by consensus.

What's the difference between critical thinking and any other type of thinking? Basically, thinking's an act of coming up with, or processing, ideas. Critical thinking, then, must mean doing something with any ideas you come up with. But doing what?

Among the possibilities: creating new ideas, having flashes of insight, problem-solving, retrieving facts and skills, knowing the meaning of what you read or see or hear, weighing alternatives to decide something. There seems to be an endless array.

Then, there are the processes—deductive and inductive reasoning, logic, use of proof. I'm sure there are more ways to generate and use ideas than I can elaborate. So I'll have to choose, and it should be something which makes sense in a classroom. After all, teachers are expected to help students think clearly and carefully. Perhaps this is what they believe critical thinking to be.

In making a choice, I'll pass on the possibilities which I mentioned two paragraphs above, They're either too closely related to subject-fields to be seen as general in nature, or are too esoteric or difficult. For example, I exclude creative ideas, or sudden flashes of thought, since I don't see how these can be part of a predetermined process. So I'll look to the four I listed last—deductive and inductive reasoning, logic, and proof. And I'll pass on the last two also, since proof is so identified with geometry that many non-math teachers don't see it as their responsibility, and formal logic seems to me to be a subject in itself.

This leaves me with deductive and inductive reasoning. To me, the latter is the more natural. We live in the here-and-now, and when an experience is repeated often enough, we tend to generalize. However, we often do so hastily, or with insufficient thought. "Jumping to conclusions" is part of the language. So this process is one which should be used with care.

I'll make inductive reasoning the process I'll focus on, although it's not truly adequate as a definition of critical thinking, and it has its own definition. Still, it's a valuable tool, it's a thought process, and it ought to be capable of development in the classroom. So here goes.

Perhaps I gave up too soon, since Inductive reasoning doesn't seem much like critical thinking. Still, I think my reasoning was defensible.

Now to define it in such specific behavioral language that it will enable anyone using it to know without doubt if a student is demonstrating the ability.

I grew up with a dictionary definition of induction as reasoning from detailed facts to general principles. Even though I think this definition is now considered to be inadequate, I'll use it for our purposes. After all, we're not operating at the college level. We all know that induction proceeds from the specific to the general, such as "All the model-T Fords I ever saw were black; it's safe to say that only black ones were made."

The problem with this kind of thinking is quite apparent. Unless you actually saw every model-T ever made, you can't be sure there wasn't an exception. No matter how many specific cases you cite, they can never prove a generalization. It can only be suggested, with varying degrees of probability, according to the circumstances.

So, our challenge is to teach students to think inductively, with proper awareness of its risks. At least, they should learn not to jump to conclusions. Still, most of the research which has led to the many benefits we enjoy today dealt with hypotheses obtained by inductive reasoning.

However, none of this is the behavioral definition I need. And as I ponder the problem, my thoughts turn to transfer of training. Earlier in this book, I noted that a skill learned in one field usually will not be used in another. The ability to do inductive reasoning in biology might not qualify a person to do it in history, nor its confident use in English lead to its application to financial decisions.

So, I'm forced to narrow my focus once again. This comports with Dr. Tyler's finding so many years ago that it's insufficient merely to define an educational objective. It must be specified in a specific context. For our purposes, I'll limit our discussion to the area of English. And so, my task is to develop a behavioral definition of the competent use of inductive reasoning in the area of English. And I must do this with absolute clarity and without ambiguity.

I feel there are two contexts in English for which inductive reasoning is relevant. The first is in the material the student reads. The second is in the remarks he or she makes, either orally or in writing. So, I present the following statements as my effort to create a definition.

Students can infer generalizations about the rules of syntax and good usage from reading passages of good writing.

Students demonstrate inductive-reasoning competence in English by identifying passages where it's used by authors, and stating the level of confidence to be placed in their conclusions.

Students demonstrate inductive-reasoning competence in English by drawing generalized conclusions from specific observations of written or spoken language, and stating their level of confidence in them.

Probably there were many other possibilities.

But, as I look at what I've just written, I'm not impressed. None seems to me to be practical. So I feel I must reconsider. Still, jumping to conclusions is so common that its risks should be understood, and students should learn to do inductive reasoning.

So where to go next? If I have to choose another specific context, which one should be used? Since we're hoping to develop an ability to transfer to everyday life, we should select the subject-field that's closest to everyday life. Shouldn't that be social studies? Let's try again.

Students recognize when oral or written statements are based in inductive reasoning.

Students recognize when their own statements reflect induction.

Students are able to state the level of confidence to be placed on their conclusions about what they read or hear or say.

These seem better. I think they're abilities which could serve an individual well throughout life. So I'll try to move on. The next step is to identify what a teacher can do to engender this kind of achievement.

And again, I have a problem. As I think about the level of confidence to be placed in a generalization, I realize that I'm baffled. I'm not certain how to do this. Of course, I know that one or two cases don't warrant a generalization. "Two swallows don't make a summer." But how many swallows are needed? And is there a way to know if different kinds of observations are more or less likely to yield a broad conclusion?

To deal with such issues calls for considerably more understanding than I possess, and will require a lot of reading. But more importantly, my lack of insight suggests that teachers might have the same difficulty, and in consequence not wish to help students in this area.

So I feel I should look at some other aspect of critical thinking. And deductive reasoning comes to mind. It seems easier, too. And it occurs to me that this is the way many teachers do much of their teaching—providing principles and expecting students to apply them.

Also, this approach is central to many subject-fields, and is seen in statements of objectives for those fields. But is the learning transferable to the outside world? And if not, should transfer be made part of the subject-matter teaching?

Probably I should have considered that many persons believe that starting with generalizations and moving to applications is not an effective way of teaching.

I remember an effort many years ago to teach geometry in a way that would assure transfer of its reasoning processes to other areas of life. Students were asked to study advertisements, editorials, and political speeches, then identify any assumptions tacitly made, and decide if the statements being made were justified. The idea was promising, but the effort took considerable class-time away from geometry, and the teachers didn't feel properly trained for it. So the "Nature of Proof" project disappeared into limbo.

I face the same problem here. Many courses in math and science stress the application of generalizations, but transferring the process to real life seems remote from the course context. Our focus must be placed within a subject which is normally related to everyday life. Two such come to mind—English and social studies.

In the former, the ability to transfer the rules of grammar to one's own written and spoken English is a form of deductive reasoning applicable everywhere. However, there's so much similarity between the rules and their applications as to make good usage more a matter of memory and practice than of reasoning. So I think I'll go with social studies.

Here we have a rich field. We can identify many desirable principles, and provide opportunities for students to decide whether or not they're being exemplified. Much of what I said earlier in this book about values and habit is relevant.

Generalizations about behavior are heard all the time. "Treat others as you'd like to be treated yourself." "Be a good friend." "Honesty is the best policy." "There is no "I" in team." And et cetera. There's no end.

It should be possible to select a few which everyone thinks are important to follow in life. It should also be possible to agree on what a teacher might do to encourage appropriate behavior, and teach learners to recognize actions which breach or adhere to an agreed-upon principle.

It would be tiresome and burdensome to consider too many generalizations. The basic approach to all is similar. So I'll limit myself to a handful, and use them as illustrations. The following objectives, then, will be my focus as I plan further.

Students can identify and acquire the elements of good human relations, such as supporting the needs and interests of others, practicing constructive cooperation, avoiding confrontations, and valuing the unique qualities of everyone.

Students know the features of good work habits, and recognize when they are practiced or breached, by themselves as well as others.

Students learn the responsibilities of good citizenship—in the school the home, and the community—and can identify both good and poor practices.

I choose these three because they're intimately related to how a school functions, with its need for good group interaction, successful learning procedures, and constructive behavior. But the statements are equally applicable to life beyond school, with the friendships, work, and home responsibilities of the boys and girls.

But I seem to have gotten far away from my original goal of planning to help students gain the ability to do critical thinking. Yet I'm not so sure. As I reflect on this matter, and ponder how teachers might view it, I've come to believe that probably any careful thought process intended to accomplish something—with guidelines for avoiding haste, side-issues, contradictions, and over-generalizations—might be called critical thinking. I'm comfortable with the belief that achievement of any of the three objectives I formulated will meet these criteria.

I'm not satisfied with the analysis I produced here. I feel I allowed myself to drift into an emphasis on starting with generalizations, followed by expecting students to apply them—a widely criticized approach. But my original commitment made me continue.

Of course, what I've done so far is still too abstract to be a working guide. I may have avoided the vagueness of over-sweeping generalities, but I must be much more specific if I'm to be helpful. For instance, good work habits in education have many working parts— careful scheduling, looking ahead, minimizing distractions, storing materials, note-taking, listening carefully, and others that don't come to mind at the moment. Every objective has to be defined behaviorally in detail if it's to be addressed successfully.

And that's my next job. I have to focus on what the teacher is seeing when the students are working, discussing, asking questions, or just being kids.

The criteria. This is where the rubber meets the road. It's all very well to have noble goals and high-flown objectives, but without objective measures for what you attempt, you're flying blind, or at least without full vision. You're plagued with uncertainty, guesswork, and subjectivity.

There are two stages involved at this point. The first is to decide which behaviors best reveal a learning, and determine what instruments and procedures are needed. The second is the actual development or procurement of instruments. These two stages interact, and there may be overlap in the process.

I now have the task of translating my objectives into something concrete, and it's not easy. Each of the three objectives I've listed above is complex, with many elements, and operative in many contexts. So, once again, I need to simplify. Since the challenge in one area bears similarity to that in another, I'll develop only one of the three.

I'll not use work habits since it's somewhat simpler than the others. Both social relations and good citizenship are more complex than the organization of an individual's work patterns. And of these two, I find social relationships more complex, more vital, more interesting, and more challenging than citizenship. So social relations it is.

Let me bring the statement back, so I can examine it

<u>Students can identify and acquire the elements of good human relations, such as supporting the needs and interests of others, practicing constructive cooperation, avoiding confrontations, and valuing the unique qualities of everyone.</u>

This objective can be divided into three parts: knowledge, skills, and habits.

The "knowledge" part includes: 1) challenges presented by social interaction, 2) definition of needs and interests, 3) methods for identifying these, 4) practices of good social interaction, 5) definition of constructive cooperation, 6) techniques for avoiding confrontation, 7) ways in which people are unique.

Additionally, the learner can be expected to acquire the following skills: 1) identifying the needs and interests of others, 2) dealing with these constructively, 3) cooperating effectively in group work, 4) ability to avoid confrontation. Each of these four areas of competence is complex.

I could, and probably should, have gone into more detail, with a greater number of specifics.

But more than knowledge and skill is required. We hope that the learnings become part of everyday living. It's one thing for a student to show knowledge and demonstrate skill upon demand. It's another to practice it of one's own volition, and when no evaluator is watching. In other words, we don't want students just to develop a certain ability, we want them to internalize it to the point that it becomes part of their personality, and is displayed habitually. In brief, we want them to develop habits.

Now, as I look at the foregoing, I feel overwhelmed. I've gained a whole new appreciation of what I've undertaken. Not only did I narrow the concept of critical thinking to an emphasis on deductive reasoning, but I analyzed the latter to the point where it became a focus on effective social relations. Then I went on to define social relations as a body of knowledge, abilities, and habits.

At every step, I was forced to choose, from among many possibilities, a smaller number on which to concentrate. The upshot is that, although a formidable challenge remains, it's part of a much wider universe. I've come to the conclusion, which I'm sure most would say is obvious, that helping children become mature, effective human beings is far more complex than I'd realized. And so much of what we do in schools is based on incidental attention, guesswork, and accident.

I'll repeat myself, and note that I should probably not have allowed myself to get so far afield from my original intention to focus on critical thinking.

Still, I feel obliged to do my best, and to continue.

As for the body of knowledge essential for good human relations, these are concepts not unlike the generalizations subject-matter teachers deal with regularly, although the area is less well defined than any subject field.

Of course, it needs to be broken done into many specifics (e.g., listing the many challenges presented by social interaction). To do this comprehensively and with validity would require us to canvass the professional literature, review our own experience, and do considerable reflection. Just one of the tasks, that of identifying the challenges of social interaction, all by itself, might well demand the time and work of an entire college course, or even more than one.

Achievement of knowledge related to social interaction, though, can be determined in the same ways as learning in subject fields, namely, by using assignments, tests, and other student performance. I'm not going to review what 's already well known.

Let me instead proceed to the skills and abilities expected of students. To do this I shall review a statement I made earlier.

"The learner can be expected to acquire the following skills: 1) ability to identify the needs and interests of others, 2) dealing with these constructively, 3) cooperating effectively in group work, 4) deftness in avoiding confrontation. Each of these four areas of competence is complex."

There are undoubtedly more than those I listed.

I'll start with the first, the "ability to identify the needs and interests of others."

How do we identify? We can of course ask. But can we trust the answers? People may know what their interests are, but may not be aware of all their needs. Or if aware, may be unwilling for a number of reasons to acknowledge them openly.

Let's define interests. These can be of several kinds, and can be held at various levels of intensity. An interest in the welfare of the disadvantaged is certainly different from one in literature, gardening, or mountaineering. We can't deal with too wide a range, so we need to narrow (once again). Probably, we should concentrate on interests which are widely shared, or are of particular importance to children and youth.

I assume that there's no great problem in identifying interests, by watching what people choose to do of their own choice, or listening to what they talk about, or just asking them. And we can ask them either orally or with a checklist. I'll not pursue this matter further.

But we're also concerned with reactions. We want reactions when interests are discussed, but we don't want those which ridicule, condescend, or are rude or hateful. Therefore, we need to note instances of behavior in any assessment we make, "Derides a statement as silly (or babyish, or stupid, or bigoted)." "Speaks favorably about another's interest." I'll develop this approach further when I create an evaluation instrument.

This is undoubtedly an oversimplification of an enormous area. But I had to start someplace.

More difficult is the identification of needs. Again, let's define. Aside from the normal physical needs everyone has, and the routine needs of daily life, which ones are important? I can think of several: 1) to be with people, and feel close to them; 2) to be loved; 3) to feel worthwhile; 4) to accomplish; 4) to be free from aggression. There are doubtless many more. We need behavioral definitions of each of these. We also need to look at negative reactions to perceived needs.

Some of the above, however, might be sabotaged by fears and anxieties within the individual, sometimes buried below the level of consciousness. Or sabotaged by the person's own behavior. If deep-seated, these are not appropriate for classroom treatment, save for simple efforts to improve unconstructive behavior. They may well require professional help, and every class may have members with serious problems.

Again, I'll deal with only one item, the first on the above list, "the need to be with people, and feel close to them." This need is near-universal. It's revealed by many kinds of actions: invitations, tagging along, asking to be involved, hanging out, and others. I'll use my best judgment to choose behaviors which indicate this need, and create a usable checklist.

My previous comment can be repeated with redoubled emphasis. I'm clearly involved in a most complex area.

Now I come to constructive cooperation in groups. This has several elements, among them: doing one's share, participating in planning, building on the ideas of others, producing work on time and as agreed, and neither trying to dominate nor accepting domination by anyone else. All this is visible behavior, easily seen in whole-class discussion and activities, but hard to observe in smaller groups working concurrently and independently. Still, the effort must be made, since an ability to work cooperatively with others is of great value throughout life.

Of course, there's a negative side. Group members may try to take over, talk past one another, fail to consider the ideas of others thoughtfully, not do their share, or produce hasty or ill-prepared work, possibly not on time. All these are part of the teacher's responsibility to observe and help.

I face a monumental task. I must define the skills and abilities I've described, specify behaviors which reveal them, and formulate instruments and procedures.

Even so, this area is more manageable than the previous one.

But there's still another ability to examine, that of avoiding confrontation. I don't see how anyone can minimize the importance of this, with all we read about road rage, bar fights, violence in families, bullying at school. The ability to calm things down, or at least walk away from a stressful situation, should be part of everyone's repertoire.

What's involved? First, is not losing one's temper when insulted, ridiculed, or threatened. It's also not retaliating when hit or attacked, and unafraid to be thought cowardly. Mostly, though, it means keeping a cool head, or at least being able to think clearly amid a maelstrom of emotions. What a tall order! Especially for young people who have not fully matured.

Soon I'll discuss trying to help students do this. Right now, I want to examine how to identify individuals who might, and those who might not, succumb. We certainly can't provide confrontational incidents in the classroom, but we can get a reading on students' proclivities. For example, how aggressive is a student's customary behavior? We might observe, "Contradicts others aggressively."

Other possible indicators of how likely individuals are to get into a confrontation: their quickness to take offense, their difficulty in seeing someone else's point of view, their readiness to say things which might offend, their sensitivity to criticism, their quickness to anger. Of course, these might or might not be predictors. But they should be studied. Only through careful observation of outcomes can we improve our ability to predict. All the above suggest at least a likelihood that a person might not avoid confrontation.

\Without a doubt, many of the preceding qualities reflect innate aspects of a person's personality, and may not be subject to much change. Still their existence can be observed.

But we should also look at the opposite—evidence that an individual might be able to steer clear of confrontation. "A soft answer turneth away wrath" is one indicator. Anyone able to speak positively in a stressful situation has a real asset. Other desirable qualities are a calm demeanor, a tendency to reach out to others, and the ability to see their viewpoint. Such behaviors should be looked for, just as one watches for negative indicators.

The final element in the objective I've selected is "valuing the unique qualities of everyone." Frankly, I don't know how to determine this, even by observing behavior. Individuals may very well act appropriately toward other persons out of a wish to be polite or to conform to expectations. Do they truly see the worth of others? Possibly this issue is one of semantics more than one of practical significance. Maybe we should be glad for constructive behavior without worrying about what it says about the inner person.

Still, we want to help students learn that every individual is unique, and possesses qualities which are of value. We should try to ascertain through observation and conversation the extent to which they have internalized such beliefs.

There are always areas which we don't feel prepared to address. This may well be one of them.

The instruments. The only practical way to determine students' abilities and habits in social interaction is through observation of their behavior. Although there have been many attempts to devise pencil-and-paper instruments for predicting people's performance in various areas, the data they yield are not very persuasive. The screening devices often used in the job-application process illustrate this.

Further, there's considerable doubt among parents and teachers about the wisdom of subjecting students to a procession of formidable instruments imported from the outside. And the focus of these may not comport well with similar objectives, as defined by a given school, and which may change from year to year. It doesn't seem feasible to rely upon such materials to assess non-subject-matter objectives.

We're left with making our own. I'll look at the three areas I've already selected: 1) identifying the need to be with people, and feel close to them, 2) constructive cooperation, 3) avoiding confrontation.

My challenge is: 1) to identify specific behaviors which reveal or preclude these abilities, 2) to describe the behaviors in such clear-cut fashion that no observer will be in doubt as to whether or not they've been seen, and 3) to provide a way to note how frequently the behavior occurs.

After much reflection, and many false starts, I've come up with three checklists, plus a set of instructions for the observer. They should be used with caution, since they're nothing more than one person's highly subjective effort. Anyone interested in them should make his or her own judgment about their value and validity.

(Author's Note: I must now confess that at this stage of my planning I deviated from my professed practice of reporting every false start. There were too many scribbled versions before I settled on the checklists. I struggled with the selection of items, the phraseology to use, as well as the format. These abortive efforts are not described since I don't feel they'd be useful to anyone. Let me just say that they were numerous.)

As I look at what I've prepared, I feel great dissatisfaction. When I eventually critique my work later, I shall have much to say about the shortcomings of what I've created. It must be viewed as merely a beginning of a long process.

The Need to Be with People

Reaches out to isolated people.
    Initiates conversation.
    Invites them to participate.
        "Is anything wrong?" "Let's do this together."

Looks for newcomers and people who seem to be alone.
    Initiates conversation.
    Invites them to participate.
        "Can I help you?" "Would you like to join us?" "I'm
        Cathy. Welcome to the neighborhood."

Notices quiet and withdrawn people.
    Initiates contact with them
    Expresses interest in their interests
    Invites them to participate
        "What would you like to do?"
        "We're going to the mall. Want to hang out?"

Is indifferent to strangers, sad, lonely, or withdrawn people.
    Does not participate when others reach out.
    Expresses lack of concern about them.
        "Who cares?" "It's up to them."

Shows unawareness of others' needs.
    Doesn't notice anyone else's efforts
        "Who? " "So what? " "Not me" or something similar.

Rejects others.
        "I don't care." ""They're no good." "It's their own fault."
        "They just don't belong here."

Tries to help people obviously in need.
"I think she's hungry." ""Would you like a share of this?"
"Mrs. Johnson broke a leg. She needs help."

Avoids helping people obviously in need.
"It's useless to try." "It's up to them."
"There's public help."

Constructive Cooperation

1. Reacts positively to ideas of others.
    (e.g., "That's good." "Let's go with that."
    "I can build on that.")

2. Reacts negatively to ideas of others.
    (e.g., "That's dumb." "How can we do that?"
    "I have a better idea.")

3. Tries to reach consensus.
    (e.g., "Let's brainstorm." "Let's take turns."
    "I'll list everyone's ideas.")

4. Tries to impose own ideas.
    (e.g., "Hey, listen to me." "I know I'm right."
    "I've looked it up.")

5. Reaches out to others.
    (e.g., "You're so good at this." Let's do this
    Susie's way." "Jim's the best organizer.")

6. Is self-absorbed.
    (e.g., "I've got to get an A." "Mike will get us
    all a bad grade." "Why did Mary get a B?")

7. Accepts leadership.
    (e.g., "I'll do what you ask," "I'll be on time."
    "You can count on me.")

8. Takes control.
    (e.g., "You do this, you do that, etc." "I've got it
    all planned." "I've made a list for everyone.")

9. Is agreeable.
    (e.g., "We're going great." "What a good group."
    "Thanks for helping me.")

10. Is disagreeable.
    (e.g., "I won't do that." "That's not fair."
    "I've got the most to do.")

11. Is flexible.
    (e.g., "I can take that one," "I'll switch if you
    need me to." "I'll fill in.")

12. Is inflexible.
    (e.g., "I won't do any writing." "I can't give an oral
    report." "I'll do it my way.")

Avoiding Confrontation

1. Expresses anger openly.
   Quickly takes offense when criticized.
   Slaps desk or slams books or doors closed.

2. Directs aggressive remarks or hostile actions toward others.
   Makes comments about people's deficiencies.
   Elbows others out of the way.
   Makes dismissive comments about others' remarks.
   "What a dumb thing to say." or "What do you know? "

3. Refuses to accept others' opinions.
   Argues instead of discussing differences of opinion
   Argues when corrected by teachers
   "That's crazy." "You're just plain wrong."

4. Is noisy and disruptive in class.
   Interrupts and talks over others already talking.
   Interrupts the teacher.

5. Orders people to do or not do this or that.
   "Get off that swing." "Me first." "Leave me alone."
   "Shut up!."

6. Is calm when the object of aggression, or maligned in any way.
   (told he or she is dumb or stupid.)
   (called by an ethnic slur.)
   (ridiculed for some physical characteristic.)

7. Accepts disappointment without anger.
   Reacts positively when given an unwanted assignment.
   Accepts cancellations and delays without complaint.

8. Tries to mediate disputes.
   > Helps separate fighters.
   > Tries to make heated remarks calmer.

9. Defends anyone unjustly attacked.
   > Clarifies misunderstood remarks or actions.
   > Suggests positive alternatives to aggression.

Instructions for Checklists

Each checklist exists in two forms. One is to be used for recording observations, with a space for a check mark each time an observation is made. The second is to consolidate the observations recorded on the first form, and show their frequency.

Many behaviors on the lists are followed by examples of remarks or actions associated with them. Anything heard can be compared with the examples given, to determine if the two are essentially the same, or of equivalent effect. Likewise, specific actions can be similarly compared. If there is any doubt in your mind about an observation being consistent with an item on a list, do not record it. Observations can be made wherever students appear in a normal situation—the classroom, the hallway, the lunchroom, the gymnasium, the playground.

After an agreed-on period of time, these observations can be combined, and recorded in the second form, which will attempt to show customary behavior. Its format has columns with the following headings: S/N - Smt - 1/2 - Frq - U/N (Abbreviations as follows: S/N - Seldom or Never; Smt - Sometimes; 1/2 - Half the Time, Frq - Frequently; U/N - Usually or Never). An 'x' is to be placed in the appropriate column for each item.

It should be noted that the two extreme patterns of behavior are difficult to determine, especially in a short period of time. The headings, "Sometimes" and "Frequently," will probably appear most often. "Half the Time" should be used rarely, to reflect true uncertainty of whether the observed behavior belongs on the high or low side.

The consolidated lists should provide an ongoing picture of a student's habitual behavior or lifestyle. It should probably appear once a semester, and not more often. Even once a year is acceptable. The results should be reported to parents.

As I review the checklists I've created, I note that I never settled on one format, nor did I make any effort to balance observations between positive and negative behaviors. Also, I could have given more and better examples. I'll say more about this when I do a critique.

Although I critique the checklists later, I'd like to add one or two comments immediately. First, I didn't know how many items it was desirable to include. Or whether there should be a balance between positive and negative behaviors, and in what order they should be placed. Finally, I also had difficulty deciding if my language was specific enough.

But it's time to go on to implementation. Now that I've set up an assessment process, such as it is, the next stage is to do something that will call for its use.

Next steps. I'm not going to propose specific classroom procedures or units to try out, since there are so many possibilities, and all who seek to improve a school's program have both the right and the obligation to select their own focus.

Instead, I'll present a few possibilities, to illustrate the kind of study which might require checklists like those I've prepared. For each of the three areas of focus, here are some thoughts which might be considered.

1. The need to be with people

i) Using the checklist, ask the class to describe anonymously their own behavior, consolidate the responses, and have students interpret the findings and suggest procedures for helping others.

ii) Ask the students to brainstorm ways of helping lonely people, and note if behavior changes.

iii) Create profiles of persons with various behavior patterns, and have students identify the needs which are revealed and how to help.

iv) Create or find a story about the struggles of a young person seeking to be accepted, and have students plan how best to provide help.

v) Assign a project whereby students anonymously reveal their own feelings of acceptance or non-acceptance, and have the class plan around the results. Protect anonymity by exchanging materials between classes, so that no one considers the reports of fellow class members.

2. Constructive cooperation

i) Have a group plan openly in front of the class, and note good practices, as well as possible additional ones.

ii) Experiment with having a teacher sit in on groups which are engaged in planning.

iii) Ask groups to self-report anonymously, using the checklist.

iv) Make a videotape of a group at work, none of whom are known to the class, and have students critique what they see.

v) Do some whole-class planning.

3. Avoiding confrontation

i) Role-play a potential confrontation, and ask students to decide how it should be handled.

ii) Get counseling assistance for students whose observed behavior suggests the possibility of confrontations in the future.

iii) Have class brainstorm how confrontations occur, and what might to done to defuse a stressful situation.

iv) Assign a project to collect reports of confrontations in the news, and obtain information about how they occurred.

v) Develop plans for counseling any students who participate in confrontations.

None of the above suggestions is more than a hint. Going forward with any of them, or with any other effort, will require the planning of specific classroom practices. And student behavior should be observed and recorded after any major endeavor, to determine if changes have occurred. Competent evaluation is central to all efforts to innovate, as is the consensus of all involved in the study. Detailing this is beyond the scope of my efforts, since it requires knowledge of a school situation and the personnel involved.

Now I'll suspend my stream-of-consciousness approach, and return to a more conventional form of presentation.

Advice on using this report. I've tried to show what can be done by persons without specialized training or assistance. My next, and final, section will be a critique of the study from as high a professional standard as I can manage. Right now, though, I want to make some encouraging remarks to those who have come this far.

First, I hope you're inspired to be more conscious of the areas I've considered, and that you look at students with greater precision, encouraging good behavior and discouraging poor. I know you're already doing much of this, but go further than you have in the past.

You certainly don't have to limit yourself to the areas I focused on. The field of observable student behavior is wide enough to encompass almost any action you might be interested in.

But if the areas I chose appeal to you, why not try your hand at improving my checklists? Choose one that interests you, read my items, and change anything you think can be improved, as well as add or subtract items according to your best judgment. Then try it out by systematically observing some students, to see if you get a better insight into any of them.

Since my checklists are only a first draft, and represent samples from a wide universe, they should be vigorously reviewed, to answer such questions as the following: Does each item represent behavior which is truly related to the ability stated in the title? Are the remarks and actions provided in the item consistent with one another and with the item's basic thrust? Is it necessary to change any of the wording to make it clearer or more realistic?

The selection of behaviors to be included in a checklist for observers must be based on the experience of many persons, not just one individual. And any term, like "Listens carefully," "Is supportive, " or "Reaches out" must mean the same thing to everyone. I've already noted that such generalized constructs are highly subjective. The only way to get consensus about behaviors reflective of them is through extensive discussion and much trial and error.

If a checklist survives this initial review, it can be tried in a real situation. But if two or more observers of the same situation, using the same list, obtain different results, the instrument needs revision. The goal is a device which gets the same result in the same circumstances, regardless of who uses it.

And if the profile of a student, as determined by a checklist, does not match the consensus of discerning persons who know the student well, the procedure requires reexamination. Either the behaviors specified in the instrument do not adequately reflect the ability in its title, or it's measuring something other than what it's supposed to.

You should then reexamine the items in the instrument, compare them with a careful rethinking of the desired outcome. Of course, this analysis, called checking the validity, can quickly take a classroom teacher too far afield. Yet it's important to keep the observation process as effective as possible.

If you can't see any discrepancy, you can still relax, knowing that even if you're not sure what it is you've measured, you know it's at least some type of constructive behavior. You might want to rename it or redefine your objective, but it would still be something positive. This is like the persons who try to avoid the challenge of first defining intelligence and then trying to prove it's truly quantified by their test results, by saying, "Intelligence is what is measured by an I.Q. test."

And if a result yielded by an instrument disagrees with an informed consensus, there are two options. The first is to get expert help. The second is for teachers to move on, doing the best they can. There's still the real possibility of obtaining positive outcomes.

Perhaps I should advise you to refrain from naming at the outset any attribute you seek to influence, since the validation process is so difficult. Why not start by simply listing behaviors that appear desirable to you, and seek evidence on how well they can be successfully encouraged.

Spending time and effort on improving insights into students' behavior might well serve as a starter for serious planning of a new program. The next step would then be a careful experiment, and any such effort should involve one or more of the following: 1) thoughtful consideration of which aspect to explore; 2) canvass of the views of your colleagues and the professional literature, 3) planning a study and creating the evaluation to be used in it. with as much care as you can manage; 4) conducting the study and incorporating your findings in your future activities. if you plan as a group, work endlessly to gain consensus. At the very least, this can be a good form of in-service education.

And now I've completed this account of my struggles with critical thinking. You'll have similar struggles too if you tackle something challenging. But don't be afraid to struggle. Most educational improvement comes only after many people make many efforts, most of them disappointing. And if you think I should be disappointed with what I achieved in this effort, you're absolutely right. I am. It was difficult, full of surprising turns, and generally not well done.

But I reported it with all its warts, to show the surprises, hard choices, and changes to be expected when planning something new. I also wanted to show that a poor result may have within it the seeds of a better one next time. It calls for further development, to increase the confidence to be placed in the results. Therefore my final piece of advice is: keep striving.

Critique. Before you say it, let me be the first. What I did is not very good, with a number of faults. In fact, one reader, after finishing it, said it showed why teachers should not do research. But, as you know from my earlier discussion of action research, I resist this point of view.

I should probably have put in additional time and thought before signing off on any aspect of my study. In consequence, I'm somewhat embarrassed by what I finished with. It certainly has all the defects of a start. It also has the shortcomings that result from not using specialized assistance.

It reveals the stumbling blocks and false starts a group of innovators may experience, and shows how haste, side-issues, over-generalizations, and contradictions can impede a project. I hope it also shows that people can make progress regardless of difficulties, and should not let themselves become too frustrated or lose hope for future success.

I expect to receive at least five major criticisms: 1) I didn't do what I set out to do; 2) there's too much subjectivity; 3) the checklists don't meet professional standards; 4) there was no real effort to create an appropriate experimental study; and 5) it was poorly written. All of these have some justification, and I'd like to discuss them. I'll try to avoid defensiveness, although I shall try to show how and why certain of these situations arose.

1. I started out to study critical thinking, and ended up with something which appears to be totally different. Many people, probably most, don't think of critical thinking as a skill of social interaction. I certainly didn't when I began. I described how my views changed as I went along, but would like to say something further.

There's no doubt that I wandered from my original intention. But, since there's no consensus on what critical thinking means, doesn't that mean an individual can define it, so long as he or she doesn't go too far afield? Did I do that? I'll leave it for you to judge, saying that I came to conclude that no area of life is more in need of careful thought than social interaction.

Still, each time I narrowed my task represented a moment when I wasn't very happy with the consequence. And I feel the areas I ended up with—need to be with people, constructive cooperation, avoiding confrontation—do not command the same level of interest as critical thinking.

In the real world, those who start out to do something about critical thinking would probably stop short of going as far afield as I did. If they'd feel too much off-track, they might keep searching for some area more clearly related to the original focus. I could have done this, and have started over, but I was fascinated by how ideas seemed to have a life of their own, and how they lead in surprising ways. Probably I allowed this to go too far. Was it useful to the reader to see this happen? I don't know.

A corollary to this criticism notes that I settled on deductive reasoning as a focus. Does this mean that dealing with needs, cooperation, and avoiding confrontation represent deductive reasoning? I could, and probably should, have reflected on this point as I went along.

My response is, yes, I do believe this. We tend to apply generalizations when we seek to improve social skills. We say, for example, "Keep an open mind," or "Constructive cooperation involves being supportive of people." These are generalizations we hope individuals will turn into specific practices. For both teachers and learners, the challenge is to learn how to do this.

In brief, the first criticism is certainly valid. The comments I made in response are not intended to defend myself, but to open a window on the complexities of a challenge like the one I undertook.

2. I showed too much subjectivity in much of the material. I plead guilty. Clearly, what I did was based on my own thoughts and experience. I tried to make this clear several times, but probably not often enough.

The checklists put this in sharp focus. I chose the elements I believed were related to the title of each, as well as the behaviors I saw as indicators. You may disagree with a number of my decisions. This shows that what I did is the beginning of a long process. I can't help but feel though that subjectivity is always at work when trying to move beyond what is widely accepted. Which leads me to the third criticism.

3. The checklists are not up to professional standards. This is dead right. They aren't. Much more was needed. Looking at instruments already created would have helped. So would a careful review of the professional literature to find what had already been done, what had been discovered, and what was being suggested. At the very least, reading up on techniques for observing and recording behavior would have improved matters.

Perhaps the above represents my limitations as an educator long removed from intensive contact with the world of youth and the pressures of the profession. Higher standards would have required vastly more effort and research than I put in. It would also have involved extensive tryouts.

Regarding checklist specifics, three areas are sharply in need of improvement: 1) inconsistency in the format; 2) the language of students' supposed remarks; and 3) the use of the "S/N - Smt - 1/2 - Frq - U/N" structure The truth is that I stopped when I did because I saw diminishing returns in continuing further.

I couldn't come to any conclusion about the item format I preferred, and decided to leave it up to the reader. And I had to recognize the likelihood that the supposed language of young people might reflect the speech of prior years more than that of today.

The "S/N - Smt - 1/2 - Frq - U/N" format deserves some comment; including several legitimate criticisms. Subjectivity is the first. Almost certainly, observers will have different parameters in mind.

I can illustrate this by telling what I sometimes did when teaching measurement. I'd ask the class to close their eyes, and raise their hands when I asked in succession if they thought the table at the front of the room was very short, short, long, or very long. Almost invariably, I received votes for every one of the four alternatives. Even a simple physical construct like "length" doesn't mean the same thing to everyone. What does this say about such terms as "Seldom" or "Frequently?"

Then there's the use of an uneven number of levels (5), instead of an even number (say, 4). The problem with an odd number is that it's too easy for an observer to use the middle rank if he or she wants to avoid the hard decision. But a true fifty-fifty is comparatively rare. Using an even number forces an observer to make a choice between the high and low side, and decide if behavior trends one way or the other.

Finally, there's the issue of whether the differences in frequency levels represent gaps of consistent size. For instance, is it a harder shift for an individual to move from "S/N" behavior to "Smt" behavior than it is to move from "Smt" behavior to "1/2," or from "1/2" to "Frq"? It's considered desirable to make gaps between levels as consistent as possible.

4. I didn't propose any specific study, or suggest an experimental design. Perhaps I should have. But I felt I'd made so many suggestions throughout the book that I didn't need one more. There's no doubt though that consideration should be given to such matters as single-class studies, multiple-class efforts, controlled studies, and single-group experiments related to the areas dealt with in this appendix. I might also have presented hypotheses to test, classroom activities to try, or units to use.

5. Finally, let's look at the charge of careless or sloppy work. This resulted from quick decisions on my part as I went through the stages of the study, and the presentation of a first draft to the reader.

Regarding this latter point. I didn't do any editorial revision of the report. Anyone who's done much writing knows this is generally a bad idea. First drafts need extensive rewriting before they're fit to show anyone. I consciously avoided revisions, however, since I wanted the reader to experience the uncertainties and self-doubts that accompany innovation. There's no doubt that the report contains much sloppiness.

I've reported that I did do some rewriting as I prepared items for the checklists. There, I felt my early efforts were so immature and unsatisfactory that reproducing all of them would drag on endlessly, and serve only to bore the reader. Still, I don't believe the rewriting I did was sufficient to achieve the quality of result I wished.

All the criticisms I've discussed have merit. And probably others of equal validity could have been advanced. If you do something like the effort I've reported, you'll doubtless receive criticism too. More importantly, you should critique yourself, in order to improve.

I wish you well.